D1454666

The Young Haymakers

Dedicated to the memory of my mother
with love and gratitude

INTRODUCTION

This is a story of a family growing up on an Offaly farm sixty years ago when the new Irish state was a mere sixteen years in existence and the Common Agricultural Policy and EU subsidies belonged to a dim distant future. Farming methods were much different to what they are today, yet the yearly cycle has not changed and for those who love the land and earn their living from it the way of life remains the same. Although my path in life took me away from farming, those days at home are etched on my memory forever and I can still feel the summer breezes and winter rains that swept down from the Slieve Bloom mountains.

My father died in 1934 aged forty-two leaving my mother to run a farm of eighty acres and rear a family of six children, four boys and two girls, ranging in ages from nine to one and a half. My sister Mary was the eldest and I was the eldest boy. Our paternal grandfather also lived with us. My mother's eldest brother, Mike Casey, to whom she owed a deep debt of gratitude, became our surrogate parent and farm manager during those crucial years after my father's death. Uncle Mike carried out the ploughing, sowing and harvesting of crops as well as running his own large mixed farm in Killeenmore three miles away where he was helped by our other two uncles, Tom and Ned.

Our farm nestled in a quiet valley at the foot of Slieve Bloom one mile west of the village of Killeigh. On the southern edge lay the heather-laden Monettia bog, the old cut-away area of which was ablaze in spring with golden yellow furze blossom. To the north five miles away was the county town of Tullamore where my mother did her shopping.

I have set the story in the year beginning September 1938 when my sister Mary was fourteen and I was going on twelve. Each chapter sets out the main farming activity for a particular month and a final chapter completes the annual cycle bringing the account back to where the cycle starts again. I have also set down the pastimes, sporting interests and good-humoured roguery which goes on in every family but which were more important back then when television was unheard of, even radio was a luxury and we had to provide our own entertainment. This record will, I trust, be of considerable interest to those working the land today. Only the weather has not changed and my description of conditions from month to month are exact and true in substance.

The novelist Maria Edgeworth once said that the reason she wrote her novels was because she wanted to set down for future generations what life was like in her own time. This is also my own modest ambition, to share with you the excitement of the arrival in our yard of Amy Hutchinson's Mogul threshing engine, the boyhood pleasure of a shopping trip with my mother to Tullamore by pony and cart and the contentment and peace that were an integral part of growing up on a farm. I hope you enjoy this story from the past when life was a great deal less complicated than it is today.

AUTHOR'S ACKNOWLEDGMENTS

There are two people in particular I must thank for the tremendous help and guidance they gave me in organising the printing and publishing of this book, Tom Martin, Willowmere, Celbridge, Co. Kildare and Patrick J. Power, 9 Maywood Ave., Raheny, Dublin. My grateful thanks also goes to John Kearney, Offaly Historical and Archaeological Society, Tullamore; Eamon Taylor and Andrew W. Murdoch, Planit Graphics; Dr. Austin O'Sullivan, Irish Agricultural Museum, Wexford; Rionach Ui Ogain, Dept. of Irish Folklore, U.C.D; Dr. Seamus Mac Philib, National Museum of Ireland, Dublin 2; Paddy O'Sullivan, Natural History Museum, Dublin 2; Gerard Casey, Kilkenny; Jarlath Glynn, Wexford County Library; Derryglad Folk Museum, Athlone; David Sixsmith, Carlow; Donal O'Sullivan, Garda Station, Tralee; Mai Branagan, Farm Tractor and Machinery Trade Association; Benny O'Gorman, DAF Ltd; Irish Farmers Journal; Dan McSweeney; Norman Alexander; Noel Garahy; my own brothers and sisters especially Christy and Mary; my children especially Rian who continually assisted me with the intricacies of the P.C. and last but by no means least my wife Peig who supported me in so many ways, and always produced the cups of coffee at the right moment, while I spent so many months in wonderful isolation in the back room.

© Tom Murray 1999

ISBN 0 9535727 0 6

Published in 1999 by Kimleigh Books, 53 St. Assam's Park, Raheny, Dublin 5.
Cover picture by Gerard Casey, Kilkenny.
Typesetting by Planit Graphics,
Marrowbone Lane, Dublin 8.
Printed by Printstone Ltd.,
Cherry Orchard Indust. Estate, Dublin 10.

x

CONTENTS

1   The Thrashin'

The rumble of cart wheels had fallen silent and the corn fields were now just sheets of stubble. All the golden sheaves safely home and fashioned into ricks and knee-stacks ready for the "thrashin' ". The "thrashin' " to us youngsters meant high excitement with visions of Armstrong Hutchinson, affectionately known to all and sundry as Amy, arriving with his ponderous black Mogul engine hauling its red and yellow threshing mill into our haggard and gangs of men coming to help: neighbours with weather-beaten faces, some wearing caps, others straw hats, but all sporting a suitable form of headgear to save their hair from the hulls and chaff and their eyes from the Autumn sun. Farm labourers sent by some of the more well-to-do farmers, who could not afford to take time off themselves. Helpers arranged by others less fortunate like the widow Farrell who had to pay a man for the day knowing that she in turn would get help when her own threshing day came round. My mother and sister Mary, wearing white aprons made from calico flour bags, washed specially for the occasion with Sunlight soap on a washboard and the usual wisp of blue added to the scalding water to give that fresh, blue-white appearance. Boiled bacon and cabbage cooked with lashings of Irish Champion or Garden Filler potatoes. Mother using a length of jute sacking, thrown over steaming hot potato pots to teem off the boiling water. The usual white enamel bucket filled with porter from the quarter barrel and an armful of blue and white striped mugs being handed round at regular intervals during the day to all the men in the haggard. The white enamel bucket of course, covered with a spotless white sheet of calico, cut from another Odlum's flour-bag which had already been subjected to the same sunlight soap and scalding water treatment as the aprons.

"You buckos better get to bed early," my mother suggested addressing me but including two of my younger brothers, Christy and Mick, "Ould Amy Hutchinson will be here at half past seven in the morning and if "the gap" isn't, open he'll drive on past it up to Con Kelly's."

The gap was the opening at the end of the haggard on to the main road, through which the threshing machine made its entry. Except at harvest time it lay impassable, continually fenced with bundles of dead whitethorn cuttings, the remnants of last year's May bush, the shaft of a horse's cart, which still had a rusty backband attached, the lids of two tar barrels and a long Scot's Pine pole across the top to add some sense of symmetry. The pole had to be rammed into the hedge at one end, and tied with barbed wire to a hazel tree at the other. Of course, the gap had not been opened since last harvest. This evidenced itself by the long strands of half-withered grass, weeds and briars which had twined their way through the dead whitethorns. Going on past performances, it seemed highly likely that one of us would endure a thorn in the finger or a gash from the barbed wire before the gap opening job was completed.

Amy Hutchinson's Mogul engine was big, black and oily with two small wheels in front and two very large wheels at the rear. Large wheels with powerful diagonal grips, wheels taller than my grandfather and a belt-drive pulley which seemed to revolve at a million revs per minute. The Mogul engine was manufactured in the United States of America by the International Harvester Company. I understand two thousand or more were shipped to Britain

The Mogul 8/16 exhibited by Norman Sixsmith of Carlow at the 1994 Steam Rally in Stradbally. This machine is almost certainly the same one owned by Armstrong Hutchinson in the late 1930's as described in the book.

while a small number found their way to Ireland, mostly to the Irish midlands. There were two models, the Mogul 8/16 and the larger and more ugly Mogul 10/20, According to Amy, the 8/16 was a much more elegant machine and it was one of these which he cherished as his proud possession It ran on paraffin oil or kerosene and was hopper cooled (no radiator). At times he fed some water into the cylinder to "help cooling and also assist the ignition," Of course, when the water boiled, steam issued from the funnel and this gave many people the impression that the Mogul was a steam engine.

  Amy Hutchinson, to me and no doubt to my brothers epitomized one of those ageless men who never had time to grow old. He had a broad friendly face with a high wrinkled brow and periodically if the mood was good a trace of a smile might be detected under the scars of wheel grease and machine oil. At best, he was an impatient man but more especially between August and November, the duration of the

3

threshing season when the smile could quickly change to an ominous frown if he or his machines were delayed. His dungarees, probably dark navy when he bought them in the Tullamore Drapery many years ago, had now faded to a greyish blue with some slightly glazed areas around the sleeves and knees. Amy Hutchinson, to us symbolized the great engineer who knew everything about machines. As well as owning the threshing mill and engine, he also had a Massey Harris reaper-and-binder and an Adriance Buckeye mowing machine with the special corn cutting fingerboard attachment and sheafing rake. He had a seed-sower, a potato sprayer and a hay bogey. It didn't end there, because his brother Dick had a model T Ford which everyone said would hold two of Father Kennedy's Baby Austin on the back seat. All things considered, he could never be seen as a man whose wrath we would want to incur. Nevertheless, we were thrilled with the knowledge that he was coming and that tomorrow we'd be thrashin'.

After a further forceful reminder from our mother that we'd look like right "gazebos" in the mornin' if we didn't say the rosary and get from under her feet on the hearth, we, together with our sisters Mary and Margaret, grudgingly slid off our chairs and knelt down. We hastily slipped caps, scarves or even a corner of the turf sack under our knees to save them from the cold and grit on the cement floor, then manoeuvred our feet as near as possible to the hot griosach in the open ash pit. The next fifteen to twenty minutes were spent reciting the five Glorious Mysteries, the Hail Holy Queen, the Litany and three Hail Marys for our Daddy's soul and several other departed relatives not to mention remaining on our knees to say our own prayers. By this stage two or three of us had made a few excursions to the

The Author seated on the Mogul 8/16 at Strandbally, 1994.

land of Nod. In the recitation of the rosary each night a certain routine was followed. Our mother recited the first Mystery, older sister Mary said the second, I carried on with the third and so on down the line to brothers, Christy and Mick. On the odd occasion, especially after a particularly tiring day, mother might announce the third Glorious Mystery just as I had finished it. This of course, caused a few giggles in the knowledge that she had also paid a short visit to dreamland and then when confronted with reality never seemed too sure how many Mysteries had in fact been completed. On such occasions if she did admit doubt and seek advice, we unanimously tried to persuade her that she had got half way through the fifth, or alternatively that the five were completed, anxious to get off our knees and the hard cement floor. Needless to say, a lot depended on her mood whether she accepted our prompts or not. However, invariably she did accede to our suggestions and carried on from that advised point with the remaining supplications.

Prayers over and after a few more veiled threats from Mother regarding the arrival time of Amy Hutchinson, we trundled off to the wooden press-bed leaving her to rake the fire. This process involved the removal of the red live turf coals from the fire grate to be covered in hot griosach and ashes in the ash pit underneath the big open fireplace. They were then taken out live again the next morning and used as the basis for a quick kindle of the new day's fire. The press-bed evolved as the common property of myself and my brothers Christy and Mick, the three eldest fellas and was a comfortable bed large enough to accommodate the three as the blue and white striped feather mattress was wide enough to overlap each side by a couple of inches. It was an ingenious piece of furniture. In the daytime folding back up into itself as an upright press with the two side wings closing in as doors, making the fixture look for all the world like a cupboard. In bed we regularly used up our final pre-sleep moments telling stories. These were not stories we had heard or read from a book they had to be totally original and composed as we went along. The best example I remember listed a farmer who decided to rear a batch of chickens for the Christmas trade but found out as the chickens grew older that most of them were cocks so the farmer pulled the tail feathers out of the cocks and sold the birds as pullets in order to qualify for the higher price.

Seven thirty, the morning of the thrashin' was introduced to all three of us by good hefty knuckles in the hips from our mother accompanied by an incessant repetition of the message, "It's nearly eight o'clock and I can hear Amy Hutchinson's engine coming up the hill at Purcell's".

The cold reality of Amy Hutchinson arriving to find the gap had not been opened created enough alarm to spur us on to the floor followed by a mad scramble for a basin of water, a towel and a bar of soap. There was nothing fancy about the soap, the same piece of Sunlight soap which had been used on the washboard the previous day to transform the flour bags into shining calico aprons. In fact the alkaline content often seemed to bleach and wrinkle our fingers if we left them in the water too long. The face washing job when unsupervised proved economic in every sense, in the time taken, area of face covered and quantity of water used. The one small basin of water always appeared to be more than enough for the three of us because of the system employed. The first one out of bed would dampen a small corner of the towel in the water, rub the Sunlight soap on the dampened area and then give the chin, cheeks and forehead a few deft and gentle rubs making sure that no soap got near the eyes and no damp cold towel near the back of the neck. The other end of the towel was then used to wipe the "washed" areas dry. The next one out of bed went through the same routine and at the end of the face washing the water in the basin remained clean enough to wash our hands.

As this was thrashin' morning, and the three of us were soon going to be covered in barley hulls and chaff, it

The Author taking out the chaff at Leslie Hutchinson's threshing, September 1995.

7

seemed most unlikely that Mother would conduct a tour of inspection especially when she knew we would all be dumped into the bathtub at the end of the day. On Sundays and Church Holydays things could be quite different. Many an embarrassing and degrading moment we lived through when, having completed our ablutions for early Mass, Mother might spot the high water line beneath the chin, the dark grey area behind the ears or brilliantine streaks on the hairline. We could then be taken unceremoniously by the scruff of the neck to have the "affected" areas scrubbed until they turned three shades of pink and maybe released with the warning "that will learn ye to do the job properly next time." However, as I said, we were thrashin' today and the chances of an inspection were remote indeed. With the short ablutions complete, we hurriedly pulled on our shirts, trousers and ganseys, stuck our feet in our knee-length stockings with the elastic garters, or more often, tied with string under the green triangular motif on the fold-down. In each case, of course, the trousers depended on a pair of gallowses for suspension and these gallowses often served to identify who owned which pair of navy-blue trousers. Christy owned the green gallowses, Mick owned the blue and I laid claim to the faded red. On this occasion we had no identification problems because Christy had a four inch nail as rear support instead of the two buttons which he burst while pulping turnips a few days earlier. The elastic had perished on one side of mine and this necessitated running repairs with an old red tie to guarantee support. We then donned the final items of working gear in the form of hob-nail boots which were purchased after last year's thrashin' and now languished in various stages of repair. Some had patches in several locations, others new toe-caps but all had been soled and heeled more than once.

A matronly quote might go something like this - "Tommy and Mikey wore out two pairs of soles sliding on the black ice on the road outside the front gate last January, Christy cut the side out of one of his with a slane while trick-acting with Tom Casey on the bog last June and Timmy wore out two sets of toe-caps kicking stones in the front yard".

As we proceeded to lace up our boots, the motley collection of materials being used as laces - binder twine, picture-frame cord and leather fongs taken from our grandfather's size elevens - gave proof indeed, that money was scarce and no new items of footwear or clothing could be purchased until after the thrashin'. With boots half tied we clattered into the kitchen, and between the three of us, made short work of nine slices of brown homemade bread and six cups of strong tea. This morning there was no time for that mug of milk and oatmeal stirabout. Just as well, too, because mother's scaremongering of thirty minutes earlier had now turned to reality. The familiar chug! chug! chug! of the big Mogul engine and the grinding noise of the metal grips on its huge wheels could be clearly heard as it laboured its way up the slight incline at Purcell's hill where we did some of our sliding on the black ice last winter.

We raced out the back like frightened rabbits, up through the haggard and launched a blitz on the bushes and poles in the gap. And just in time too, Christy was actually pulling out the last strand of briar as the engine drew level. The three of us quickly scampered out of the way, and looked on in awe as the ponderous hulk of machinery, wheels and belts chugged its way in through the opening and down between the two knee-stacks of oats, and ricks of wheat and barley which had been carefully built a predetermined distance apart to match the width of the mill, with its pitching boards extended. Our hearts were beating fast with excitement but nevertheless, we kept a healthy distance away from the mill and engine because of tales our elders had told us about how similar engines had exploded. Cluck Dunne frightened us last year with his story about an engine he saw explode in Lennon's haggard away down in Killeenmore. He told us that as it exploded, it jumped over a rick of straw, almost touching the heads of the men making the rick, and landed right end up on the other side. As in previous years we got braver every minute and edged our way closer to the big Mogul to witness it come to a halt between the ricks. Amy Hutchinson wriggled around on his straw-filled cushion and dismounted. He proceeded to supervise his "feeder", Joe Brien, who took a heavy sledgehammer and some large, black, oily wooden wedges from the open-top tool box located diagonally across the engine underneath Amy's seat.

In the thrashin' day hierarchy the feeder slotted in second from the top giving precedence only to the driver/owner. His was no one-day job, a picked man, he teamed up with the driver, for the complete threshing season. His job demanded total concentration because he stood within inches of a high-speed revolving drum while he fed the sheaves of wheat or barley through its whirling blades to separate the grain from the straw and chaff. In John Neill Watson's marvellous book, "A history of farm mechanisation in Ireland 1890 - 1990", he refers to the feeder as "an important figure, having equal status with the driver". On the subject of "feeding", he goes on to say, "feeding was an acquired skill which required day-long concentration. It was also a dirty job as clouds of dust were constantly blowing up from the drum. It was a dangerous job, with the feeder standing in a sunken box facing the exposed revolving drum".

Joe hammered the wedges in tight against the front and rear wheels of the mill and engine. He did this to eliminate any forward or backward movement of either during the threshing operation. Next, the long black drive belt with its mysterious overlap had to be fixed in position, running from the drive pulley on the engine to the drive wheel high up on the side of the mill. According to Amy Hutchinson, this represented a particularly skilful part of the preparations. The engine had to be positioned so that its drive pulley remained in exact alignment with the drive wheel on the mill, otherwise a loss of power would ensue and the belt would continually slip off the drive shaft.

While Amy and his feeder systematically attended to all preliminaries, the "thrashin' " day helpers began arriving in ones and twos. My uncles, Mike and Tom Casey, were first on the scene, each sporting a hay fork on their shoulders. Mike had a reputation all over the parish and maybe further afield as a "topper at makin' a reek" so no doubt his job was a foregone conclusion. Tom, on the other hand operated as a jack-of-all-trades who could slot into "pitchin' shaves," "cuttin' shaves" or "carryin' straw". Next to arrive was Cluck Dunne, a small plump man in his middle fifties with a round red face, a short wiry moustache which had long since ceded its grey tint to the brown stains of porter and pipe tobacco. He was a man with a well-trained limp, a slow speaker, an excellent storyteller, exuding a real sense of humour and an infectious belly-laugh. We young lads were delighted to see Cluck's advent because that meant we'd each get an egg-cupful of porter and were guaranteed some good stories at the after-thrashin' do. Of course our mother's reaction differed totally. When she saw Cluck waddle into the yard, her comment could easily be predicted, "There wont be much done at whatever end of the reek he's at".

However, the bould Cluck left his hay fork, or as my grandfather called it, his two-grained fork, against the outside wall of the dwelling house, and stepped into the kitchen, with a hearty - "God bless all here."

Fantin Kerwin, Joe Fletcher, Jim Connolly and Pat Walsh were already seated at the freshly scrubbed pine table, finishing their mugs of "tay".

"I suppose you'll have a mug too?" my mother ventured to Cluck.

Cluck readily agreed he'd "have a drop in the hand" and followed quickly with the proviso, "Ah, but don't go to any trouble, Mrs."

This expression usually peeved my mother and raising the tone of her voice, with a hint of sarcasm, she countered, "Oh it's no bother at all."

Out in the haggard Amy Hutchinson and Joe had completed all their preparations. The powerful Mogul engine sounded out a staccato chuff! chuff! chuff! The long black drive belt criss-crossing itself halfway between the drive shaft on the engine and the pulley wheel on the mill slithered into motion getting faster and faster and periodically slapping its inner sides together as if clapping its hands in enjoyment that the action had at last begun. Now all systems were go and as the drive belt gathered speed, the drum in the mill steadily revved up to its familiar high-pitched whine. At this point my uncle Mike who had been busy laying out a base for the new straw rick, with cuttings of whitethorn and hazel mixed with dusty forkfuls of the remnants of last year's hay approached me with a grin. I knew he had nothing good on his mind especially when I saw a beet-fork in his hand. He shoved the beet-fork towards me, with the loaded and doubtful compliment "You're the best man at takin' out the chaff". Taking out the chaff had to be without doubt the dirtiest job of the day and in every haggard, on threshing day, it usually fell to some hardy young gosoon. It meant working in a confined area at the front of the mill where a wind tunnel whirled out the broken straws, hulls, chaff, dust particles and poppy seeds in an unbroken deluge. This flotsam had to be raked out to one side and the area kept clear at all times.

In order to allow me no chance of protest Mike indicated that all pitchers were in position, all stations were manned and Joe Brien, the feeder, stood awaiting the first sheaf. He rounded off his "get going" directive to me with the knowledgeable remark that I should "know how fast the chaff builds up." Suddenly the high-pitched whine of the drum reduced to a lower tone and then momentarily stalled and groaned as the first fanned-out sheaf of wheat hit the whirling steel. The two men pitchin' shaves had now taken up definite positions on the rick. The fellow at the furthest end of the rick tossed the heavy wheat sheaves back to the pitcher nearest the mill. He in turn picked up one sheaf at a time with his two-grained fork, gave it a whirl as he flicked it in to Mick Clear who was "cuttin' shaves" so that the sheaf reached the feeder right way round for entry into the drum. Within minutes, the production process became streamlined and sheaves arrived right end first all along the line. This in turn meant that Mick Clear could now slit the binder-twine band on each sheaf with one neat stroke of his specially sharpened, half-bladed kitchen knife. The handle of the "shafe cutter's" knife carried a heavy bandage of cloth tied on with binder- twine. There were two reasons for this, it gave better bulk to the handle for grip and it helped to save the sheaf cutter's hand from getting blisters.

Things were now generally buzzing. Amy Hutchinson, hovering beside his beloved Mogul, his wrinkled face sometimes showing the suggestion of a benign smile, lovingly dropped a few blobs of thick brown oil from the snipe-like spout of his oil can on to the governors and other moving parts of the engine. As the smile grew broader on his face he obviously became more content that things were going well and seemed as happy as a mother feeding milk to her baby.

Tom Casey, Danny Doolin and Pat Kelly were pitchin' shaves. Mike Casey and Fantin Kerwin engineered the new straw rick, while Joe Fletcher, Paddy Poland and Pat Purcell carried straw. Jim Connolly and Joe Condron attended to the grain-filling operation or looked after the bags as we called it. Con Kelly and Jack Mooney moved the full sacks of grain away from the mill with a sturdy hand-truck to

lie against a hedge some safe distance away. Cluck Dunne and Ned Conroy always managed to look busy and important. Their caps and dungarees already displayed a greater collection of hulls, chaff and general dust than the quality of their exertion warranted. But they were ould-timers at the game and past masters at making a

Hand truck used to move the full sacks of grain away from the mill.

one-man job look like severe strain for two. My brothers, Christy and Mick had by this time, yoked Kerry the red pony to the blue-shafted cart and busied themselves assisting Mike Cooke and Jimmie Moran in transporting the full sacks of grain from the haggard to the barn. This proved to be good fun for the two boyos, because the sacks of grain were far too heavy for them to lift and they got a "jant" on the trips to and from the barn.

Soon it would be eleven thirty a.m. on this humid autumn morning and the weather had "stayed up well." Three-quarters of the rick of wheat was pitched and threshed with an out-turn of thirty eight sacks of grain. Joe Condron reminded us that that represented thirteen barrels to the acre and as it was harvested in good dry conditions the moisture content would be low, and the grain should qualify for top price, "Tang God".

"Well hell te yer sowl, Mrs. Murray, I thought ye had forgotten us" said Cluck Dunne as my mother and my sister Mary arrived in the haggard with two enamel bucketfuls of porter, each covered with a white calico cloth.

"An how could I forget ye, Mike?" said my mother, reluctant to call him Cluck, it might sound altogether too familiar.

"An how could I forget ye, indeed?" she repeated as she handed the bould Cluck his blue striped mugful of the juice of the barley.

The ceremony of tapping the quarter barrel had taken place a short time earlier. "Tapping" the quarter barrel could not be left to any Tom, Dick or Harry. This remained a specialist's job and had to be performed to perfection so that no drop of the precious dark brown liquid might be lost. The right man for the task of course had to be Johnnie

Delaney. He arrived a little late but just in perfect time to take on this skilful act as he had done last year and the year before. Johnnie took the brass tap, then a ribbon of freshly washed jute sacking. He carefully wound the sacking around the stem of the tap working it into a spiral so that the diameter of the outside face of the spiral would barely over-run the diameter of the wooden bung in the side of the quarter barrel. Then placing the tap just above the bung and with one expert stroke of a light mallet the tap slipped into position, the wooden bung lay inside the barrel and the sacking around the brass tap ensured that no liquid escaped.

My mother and my sister Mary continued on their rounds until all workers had had their refreshments. The very few who for various reasons, resisted the contents of the enamel bucket were treated to a bottle of Williams' red lemonade. By one o'clock the complete rick of wheat and almost half the rick of barley had been threshed. The yield looked good as forecast earlier by Joe Condron. The balance of the barley rick and two knee-stacks of oats were all that remained to be threshed. No doubt dinner-time would upset the momentum but nevertheless Amy Hutchinson could be on his way to Con Kelly's before five o'clock and possibly "get in a couple o' hours for Con before dark". Indeed, the dinner did upset the momentum, because on the stroke of one Christy and Mick arrived back in the haggard, after doing a grain trip to the barn, with the news "the dinner's done." Before you could say Barley Wine, Mike Casey and Fantin Kerwin the two rick makers, stuck their hay-forks into the golden straw, wiped the dust and grit from their foreheads and clambered down the steps of the rickety, wooden ladder.

"Why the hell don't ye get that yoke fixed?" said Fantin, "I nearly broke me leg on it last year."

Fantin was, of course, speaking to everybody and nobody so nobody answered. For these two men who had been foundering around on the soft wheaten straw while making and "walkin' in" the rick the sense of solid earth beneath their feet felt good indeed. Tom Casey and Pat Kelly who were pitchin' shaves soon followed suit as did the straw carriers Joe Fletcher, Paddy Poland and Pat Purcell.

Suddenly you could almost hear the hush that enveloped the haggard, as the old Mogul clanked to stillness and the loud drone of the mill gave way to the cheerful chat of the men discussing and comparing their jobs during the morning's toil. In twos and threes they sauntered down the haggard towards the dwelling house taking their time as if knowingly trying to allow the kitchen mechanics a few extra, valuable moments to sort out the plates, or the seating arrangements. On the way to the kitchen they had to pass the cobbled yard at the end of the house and this presented the opportunity to stomp their hob-nail boots on the bare stones and shake off the remaining hulls and straws from their footwear, dungaree and trouser legs. Passing the wooden pump in the front yard they briefly stopped to rinse their hands and shook them briskly in the air "to dry off the big drops" as my uncle Mike said while at the same time flicking a few drops into my eyes.

The moment of truth had now arrived for my mother. A troupe of hungry men had to be fed and she knew that as they sat down, each one expected he would be the first to be served. On many occasions throughout the year she had said to me and my brothers Christy, Mick and Tim, especially in recent years as our appetites grew stronger, "feedin' you gang is like feedin' a thrashin'." Well now for the umpteenth time in her comparatively young life she was about to take on the real thing. The settlebed had been moved from the kitchen to make room for a second table, which we borrowed from Mrs. Fletcher for the day. With spaces for three on forms on either side and a chair at each end this meant that two tables could seat sixteen bodies. The remainder of the hard core of workers would be accommodated at a larger table in the parlour. Amy Hutchinson, Joe Brien and Mike Casey were among the gang usually housed in this area as well as myself and Christy. My younger brothers Mick and Tim, were the recipients of less sympathy. In the heat of the kitchen on thrashin' day they were usually told, "Ye can take yerselves outside, and wait 'til the "min" are finished".

"God save all here," "God bless the work," "Tang God for a fine day." were the salutations, as one by one they ambled into the kitchen. With a grating of boots and a scuffing of form legs against the cement floor they each found a seat in a reasonably orderly fashion. The tables were economically set with the minimum of cutlery laid out neatly opposite each seat, knife and fork, a blue and white striped

The Allis Chalmers Engine which supplied the power at Leslie Hutchinsons's Threshing, September 1995.

mug, for fresh milk or porter with pepper, salt and mustard in the background. Thrown out on the white tablecloth in the centre of each table lay a generous pile of steaming, hot potatoes with their skins cracked open. As soon as most of the men were seated Mrs. Poland and my sister Mary busily handed out plates of boiled bacon and cabbage, each carrying two plates at a time. The banter sounded good and loud.

"They're great spuds, Mrs." enthused Jimmie Moran as he held up one of the big floury potatoes on his fork and commenced peeling it.

"Just as well we're not sittin' at Doolin's table, Jim" added Fantin Kerwin, with his infectious chuckle, "I heard he ate seventeen spuds at Colton's thrashin' last Friday."

"Ah, sure that was probably just for starters" said Pat Kelly, "I believe he put away twenty at Corbett's o' Killeigh last year."

"God, ye're all fierce smart" countered Danny, "If ye were half so bloody smart at makin' a reek Fantin, your end wouldn't be slippin'."

For a professional rick maker like Fantin, whether making a rick with sheaves or new straw, nothing but nothing could be more humiliating than to be told by a pitcher that one end of the rick was slipping. Slipping, meant the rick bulged and sagged in one specific area and when this happened, if not spotted and rectified early, then it usually ended in a strawslide or total collapse.

"Don't mind Kerwin and Kelly" suggested Mike Cooke, "they' re ony gettin' it up for you, Danny."

"Gettin' it up for me is right" continued Danny - "it's a pity Kelly couldn't get up a shaggin' shafe now an' agin an' give Tom Casey a dig out; Mick Clear is shiverin' with the cowld, up on the mill with nothin' to do."

"Well bedad I'll change me job with anyone that believes that" said Mick, "I've a pain in me showlder from shaves hoppin' off it."

"Wouldn't they put years on ye listenin' to them, Mrs." suggested Pat Purcell addressing my mother, "I've often seen twice that much thrashed in half the time with good min pitchin' and carryin'."

"Well I'll have to lave you to be the judge o' that Pat, all I know is I haven't stopped goin' meself since I got up at half past six this mornin', an' I'm sure I'll still be goin' at half past twelve tonight."

That retort from Mother introduced a slight element of seriousness into the conversation. Nevertheless the good humoured jeering, joking and repartee continued unabated until justice had been done to the last potato and the last nut of boiled bacon.

Cluck Dunne foostered in the pockets of his faded work-jacket, then lovingly produced the stained remnants of what was once a richly shaded briar pipe. The metallic lid or heel-top as Cluck called it, with the two smoke holes, could scarcely cover the deeply burned erosions around the top of the bowl. The silver coloured ring at the centre of the shank, long since cracked and loose, was now missing and the plastic-like mouthpiece was neatly banded with loops of fine tea-twine to give a better grip.

"There's a few ould tusks missin' you know" said Cluck, as he tightened the twine on the mouthpiece and lapsed into one of his characteristic infectious belly-laughs. Then slowly regaining his composure, took the tail end of an ounce of Ruddell's twist tobacco from underneath the cap which he wore peak to back during the threshing season, "to keep the barley hulls from goin' down me spine." Now, the

Carrying straw away from the mill to the new rick at Leslie Hutchinsons's threshing, September 1995.

ritual of filling the pipe could begin. The dried ash from the top of the previous "smoke" he judiciously poked loose and carefully stored it in the lid or heel-top. Small slivers of plug were then chipped off with the penknife and dropped into the palm of the hand which held the ingot of tobacco. There was no guesswork about this part of the sequence, this called for real precision, because on every occasion he processed the exact quantity of tobacco to fill the pipe.

With the penknife held between the fingers of the other hand Cluck now proceeded to do a crushing or pulping job with the heel of his fist until the mixture became nicely rubbed. He then moved the bowl of the pipe to a position underneath the pile so the mixture could be expertly transferred into the bowl with downward strokes of the index finger. After the filling operation the contents were gently pressed down and the ash or heel-top added to the new pipeful. The exercise was now complete, the pipe ready for lighting. Ordinary mortals would probably produce a box of matches but not Cluck. He took the tongs in his hand, picked up a glowing red turf coal from the open fire and crushed a few tiny burning embers into the pipe bowl.

"The turf gives the tabackey a better flavour" said Cluck.

After three or four quick laboured pulls on the pipe his friendly face became enveloped in aromatic twirls of pale blue tobacco smoke, as he made his way back to the haggard and once more resumed his toils.

By this time all the other men were manning their respective stations. The engine sounded full steam ahead and the mill once more disgorged its never-ending stream of rich golden straw. With energies well revived, industry again became evident in all areas. Sheaves seemed to arrive faster on the mill table. Mick Clear cuttin' shaves had upped his tempo considerably and now collected the binder twine bands at a brisk rate. Even the straw carriers appeared to have a greater cargo in each forkful. Earlier forecasts regarding finishing time were proving accurate. By half past four the last few sheaves of the final knee-stack of oats had

Threshing at Mike Casey's (Author's Uncle) Killeenmore, in the 1930's with the actual Mogul Engine as described in the book. Dick Hutchinson, brother of Amy, is standing at the rere of the engine. (Courtesy: John Kearney, Offaly Historical and Archaeological Society, Tullamore.)

been tossed on to the mill table, slit and passed through the threshing process. However, Amy Hutchinson continued to leave the mill and engine running to clear the system of all remaining grain, straw and chaff. The whine from the free-running drum, now a high pitched monotone, in some strange way sounded sad as if lamenting the end of another episode in its threshing life. Mike Casey and Fantin Kerwin had at least, a further hour's work headin' off the straw ricks. This meant carefully drawing in the top of the rick with forkfuls of straw pulled from the butt of the rick and then bringing it to its final taper, with a layer or two of the remnants of last year's musty hay. This final seam had to be covered with old bran sacks or fertiliser sacks and then draped over with wire ropes at six or seven feet intervals. The wire ropes were held down on either side with chunks of metal, blocks of wood or any other heavy items which might be readily available.

Tom Casey and Pat Kelly now redundant because there were no more sheaves to pitch gave a hand where there seemed to be most need. With the big wheaten rick headed off, Mike and Fantin moved on to the somewhat smaller barley rick and then did a finishing off job on the butt of oaten straw. Joe Fletcher and Jim Connolly also redundant helped out loading sacks of grain and transporting them to the barn. It developed into a real case of all for one and one for all as the men moved from job to job helping each other to finish. In the meantime, Amy Hutchinson and Joe Brien had dislodged the wheel props, slipped off the drive belt, swept down the mill table and were slowly manoeuvring the ponderous cavalcade of machinery out through the gap once more and on to the main road heading towards Con Kelly's.

Although the weather had been dry and overcast all day, the evening now turned cooler, and misty rain clouds were gathering on the Slieve Bloom mountains.

"Ye can hear the Cat-Holes" said Fantin, "the evenin's bet, there'll be nothin' thrashed at Con's this evenin'."

The Cat-Holes, a term given to an eerie, moaning sound not unlike some of the cadences in the tomcat's mating call, occasionally caused by the west wind as it whistled through "The Cut" or some ravine high up in the Slieve Blooms. When the Cat-Holes sounded the phenomenon was recognised as a sure sign of rain and on this occasion it did not disappoint. Scarcely had Mike and Fantin completed the heading off jobs on the three new ricks of fresh dry straw, when the first sheets of rain, driven by a south-westerly breeze drifted in over the Slieve Blooms and quickly made their way across the broad Monettia bog down to the valley below. Luckily Mike Cooke and Jimmie Moran transported the last sacks of grain to the barn before the first droplets fell. They had completed a good job, efficiently and on time. The yield looked good, fifty eight bags of wheat, twenty six barley and twenty sacks of oats. All in all a good day's work, one hundred and four sacks of grain. Mother seemed well pleased and with the hint of a grin on her cheeks, suggested, "Maybe I might be tempted to buy new boots for ye all, but don't forget it's goin' to cost me thirteen and ninepence a pair in Duggan's corner shop, for good leather ones."

"And if ye get a pair for grandad, it'll cost ye fifteen and ninepence", said Mick, "because Tom Casey got a pair last week an' that's what he paid for them."

Although several farmers in the area traditionally arranged thrashin' dances in their kitchens or barn lofts on the night of the thrashin' we had not done so for a few years since our Dad died. Nevertheless we enjoyed good fun on the night. Our uncles Mike and Ned Casey usually stayed on after tea-time to play the melodeon or as Mike said himself, "scratch a few tunes on the fiddle." Jimmie Moran held sway as top contributor of popular ballads while Cluck Dunne filled in the intervals with his unhurried, laid-back brand of witty stories. Doubtless, all good things must come to an end. We knew the shindig was over when Tom Casey and some of the other bicycle brigade stood up and collected their carbide lamps from where they had carefully stowed them away in the morning, on the top shelf of the broad pine dresser. It was essential that the lamps should be in good working order on this wet starless night. Tom Casey added a few new chunks of carbide, tightened the under chamber, poked out the gas-jet with a safety pin, added two or three drops of water then lit the bright, blue-white flame and slipped the lamp on to the bracket of his old faithful Raleigh bike. With a hasty farewell and advising us not to come outside "or ye'll be drenched," he donned his weather- beaten cap, buttoned up a well worn trench coat and pedalled off into the night, luckily with the wind in his back for the three mile spin to Killeenmore. The rest of the revellers soon followed suit, some on bicycles and others who lived close by on shank's mare. The thrashin' had now well and truly come to an end for another year. Being close to midnight, we were directed to "say yer own prayers and get off to bed, it's too late to say the rosary."

During the following days the old Ford trucks of Tullamore malsters, Egans and Williams, shuttled to and fro collecting the sacks of grain from us and neighbouring farmers. Normally, we sold all the wheat with the exception of one sixteen-stone sack which was kept for grinding into wheaten meal at Cobb's mill. Throughout the year mother used this meal mixed with flour when baking her wholesome brown bread. Traditionally all the barley was sold but most of the oats was kept, some for animal feeding and a further supply converted into full grain oatmeal to be used in making our daily plate of stirabout during the winter months.

2   Pickin' potatoes

Sunday, the second of October soon manifested how lucky we were to have threshed the previous day. As Amy Hutchinson pulled out of our haggard on Saturday, the wind came up, rain began to fall and the "cat-holes" sounded ominous in the distance. By evening time on Sunday the wind had matured into a major storm which didn't subside until the early hours of Tuesday and caused widespread damage in the county. Trees were blown down making some roads impassable, slates ripped off roofs and corn stacks blown over in the fields. The wet and windy conditions lasted for a week, badly disrupted harvesting operations and left several families with half dry turf on the bogs. Thankfully the next few days brought a dramatic turn-about in the weather. Once again the days became bright and breezy, interspersed with many welcome hours of sunshine. Corn crops, whether in stacks, stooks or ricks quickly dried out, while harvesting again became the order of the day. Uncle Mike had somehow found time to pull the remainder of his apple crop before the storm and in his own long proven style, stored them like potatoes in a pit covered with straw and a deep layer of barely damp soil. His apples always wintered perfectly and he would often gloat, "what d' ye think o' that?" as he handed out a nice crisp, firm apple from his store, possibly as late as mid March.

October was now nearly two weeks old and oozing that pleasant smell of Autumn with its misty mornings and six o' clock sunsets. The old folk were quick to point out that their rheumatics had already reacted to the extra nip in the cool midland air. Grandfather had often proclaimed that the air in the midlands always felt cooler in the winter and warmer in the summer, than anywhere else in Ireland. Be that as it may, plenty of hard work still needed to be completed. The main potato crop was due to be taken out and pitted. During the past few days a lot of preparation had taken place. Sites were cleared for the new pits, basket handles repaired and several pony-loads of scraws had been cut and drawn from the bog. The scraws were twelve inch square sods cut approximately two inches deep from the old section of the cut-away bog. The cutter picked his patch carefully to ensure each 'scraw' sported a short growth of young heather, nicely mingled with strands of sedge and moss. These scraws were used to cover the potato pits, with the mossy sides turned inwards. Mike Casey agreed with grandfather that they were the best possible protection from frost, keeping the potatoes fresh and cool right through the winter and spring and had proven their worth over generations.

This morning he arrived early in our yard with the 'spudler' hauled by his two kind-eyed , black geldings. Mike

Spudler.
(Courtesy: Irish Agricultural Museum, Johnstown Castle, Wexford)

had harvested his own crop earlier, and Christy and I gave him three days picking and pitting. He had now come to make a start on our potato crop in the near moor. All hands were mobilised and now stood ready to carry out the plan of action agreed on the previous evening. Mike would operate the mechanical potato digger or spudler as it was universally known in the midlands. Christy had already placed two horses' carts and one pony cart at regular intervals along the headland running parallel to the first potato drills. There were four teams of two to man the four potato baskets. These teams comprised my brothers Christy, Mick and Tim, our neighbour Paddy Poland, three local youths hired for the duration of the job and myself. The baskets were home made by grandfather from thin hazel wattles, better known locally as scollops, pretty similar to those used all over the country for thatching. We helped Mike Casey make some final adjustments to the spudler. Fifteen metal grips similar in appearance to a two-inch section of an ice skate blade, had to be fitted to each road wheel and fixed in position with split-pins. These grips were never used on road journeys, they could cause damage to the road surface as well as drastically curtailing the speed of movement. Their sole purpose related to the work field during harvesting operations. Mike Casey's journey from his home in Killeenmore to our house had to be undertaken totally by road, so he obviously left this fitting job until he arrived.

The action would soon be ready to commence.

"Ho tee yah! Hob off! Woa! Woa!" were Mike's crisp instructions to two willing, intelligent horses as they strained eight powerful legs and manoeuvred this gangly machine with its menacing kicking arms, into position on the first potato drill. With the click of a lever, the sole plate slipped down into the soft earth well below the lowest depth of the drill, the kickers spun into motion and suddenly we had a spray of loose soil, pebbles, weeds, potato stalks and of course potatoes. While the spudler progressed down the drill the pickers moved into position, each team accepting responsibility for a quarter of the processed area. As the baskets became full they were emptied into the nearest cart. The younger folk had little or no opportunity to trick-act or waste time. The spudler moved at a steady speed. With one drill completed , it trundled back idle to commence the next and so on in a never ending circuit. Mike Casey, always a hard task master, just smiled wryly if he caught up on a team which had fallen behind and was making frantic efforts to finish before a new spray of flying earth covered their unpicked territory. Thankfully, this seldom happened. Teams which finished ahead of the others usually helped out their less fortunate neighbours.

Despite the fact that potato picking is indeed a back-breaking exercise, especially for adults, a thread of good fun and witty banter weaved through all conversation, as well as an undercurrent of healthy rivalry between the teams. As a precaution against frost, all carts whether full or partly full, were hauled in to the already prepared plot before darkness fell. When Christy moved to drive in the first cart, we took this as a signal that the spudler had finished for the day. Now all teams emptied their final baskets and followed the carts to the pit area situated under two large chestnut trees, in a corner of the field right opposite our dwelling house, with only the front yard intervening. This had been the habitat of potato pits since grandfather, and maybe his father before him were schoolboys. I suppose I should explain that, in the midlands, the term potato pit represented the long, low, tapering clamp of potatoes harvested by farmers, for their own use throughout the year and for seed for the following year's crop. These pits received as much tender care in the making as did the turf clamp in another season.

An October dusk had now settled over the valley and the glow of the paraffin lamp through the kitchen window, made the jingle of tea-cups all the more appealing. Although we were all hungry and reasonably tired, still a great air of diligence prevailed while we tidied the last few scattered tubers, and left a nice isosceles face on our new creation. We hurriedly covered the pit with a patchwork of old jute bags and carefully placed a mantle of scraws in position, making quite sure that no square inch remained stripped and no potato left as prey to the elements, or food for the marauding crows. Crows were very fond of raw potatoes and could often be seen in small flocks digging out partially stripped tubers from the drills with their strong beaks. Of course Mike Casey loved to cod the "gossoons" and told us during the dinner break, the story of the farmer who was persecuted by flocks of crows stealing his produce. As a deterrent, an old woman from the mountain advised him to shake salt in the furrow of each drill. This he did, and got up early the next morning to inspect his crop only to find that there were more crows than ever in his field, digging out potatoes, dipping them in the salt and eating them! Mike finished the yarn with one of his eye-watering, belly-shaking laughs in the knowledge that, once again, he had put one over on the young "fellas."

While we were tidying and covering the new pit our uncle had unyoked his team of two, carefully hanging up their "tacklings" and settling them in the stable with a vigorous rub-down, a forkful of hay and a tidy ration of oats

The Jack Snipe

to say thanks for a job well done. All the workers were now ready to make an assault on the kitchen and pay serious respects to the long awaited rasher, egg and black-pudding helped on their way with a mug of strong tea and many slices of homemade wheaten bread. Mother seemed delighted with the day's progress, twenty four drills taken out and pitted, fourteen British Queen and ten Kerr's Pink. This only left two more Kerr's Pink, eight Golden Wonder and the twelve drills of Sprys for pig feeding. Tomorrow would take care of these and still leave time to give the pits their final covering. This meant removing the temporary jute bags, substituting them with a fine sprinkle of wheaten straw and carefully replacing the bog scraws. The complete surface area could then be covered with approximately four inches of soil or clay as we always

The Red Grouse

called it, dug from shallow trenches on either side of the pit. That would finalise the harvesting of the potato crop and leave it safely stored to withstand the winter frosts, sleet or snow.

We have now reached the end of the third week in October. Birdsong is scarce except for the sweet notes of winter's foremost singer, the robin. Frosty evenings tend to

The Blackbird.

bring out the best in the blackbird as he pipes a few intense notes on his urgent trip from the haggard across the open yard to the chestnut tree beyond. The days are getting shorter and close by in the majestic expanse of the heather laden Monettia bog, we can clearly hear the grouse issuing its favourite command, "Brrrrrrrrr! Go bak! Go bak! Go bak!" High overhead in the clear night sky, the snipe, the bird that Mother prefers to call "the skygoat" wheels into zig-zag motion and bleats its goat-like cry in a staccato, Baaaaaa!

The sun had gone down red beyond the Glosh and all the weather signs were telling us that tomorrow promised to be cool and dry and a good day for Tom Casey and Paddy Poland to start pulling beet. As my brothers and I had already missed three days from school, one for the thrashin' and two picking potatoes, we thankfully could not join in the beet pulling until Saturday. The Glosh, where the name came from we are not too sure, possibly from the Irish word Glas meaning green, or green place, represented a special stretch of the Clodiagh river at the south extremity of Kelly's farm. This stretch was wide and deep, a favourite place for all the local youths to swim or dip in the warm summer months. Indeed it was not the confine of the young population. Often during particularly warm summers many bog workers who had withstood the heat of the day cutting and wheeling turf, came there to cool off when the day's work was done. The Clodiagh river meandered down from the nearby Slieve

Bloom mountains so the water remained clean and fresh. A good fishing river during the fly fishing season. It passed under Gorteen bridge a favourite haunt of the kingfisher, resplendent in its bright emerald green, chestnut and blue, and a much loved watering hole for us schoolgoers on our way home from Killurin school. Many evenings it was the cause of us being late home, after spending long glorious moments paddling and searching for pinkeens.

The red sunset had forecast correctly, morning dawned bright, cool and calm. You could even see a hint of frost on the pale green leaves of the beet crop as Tom and Paddy set to work. Tom had donned his weather-beaten overcoat or top coat as he preferred to call it, fastened at the neck with a safety pin and tied figure-tight at the waist with a stout string of binder twine. Above the hob-nail boots he wore a pair of leggings or gaiters, cut from vestiges of last year's beet-pulp bags and these too were tightly laced with binder twine. This attire offered real protection for his legs against the heavy dew as he made his way through the forest of leafy drills. Paddy was garbed in similar apparel and like Tom, preferred to wear his brown peaked cap, back to front. Both got down to business without delay, pulling the plump, arrow shaped beet roots, banging them together crisply to dislodge any excess earth and then dropping them neatly on the ridge from which they had been uprooted with leaves always hanging to the same side. Because of the rich, soft soil in that particular field, progress developed swiftly.

At the stroke of mid-day, Mike Casey who had to visit Tullamore earlier, joined Tom and Paddy and excepting the dinner break and a short respite for four o' clock tea they worked non-stop until the last vestige of light disappeared from the western sky. By noon the following day the one and a half acres of beet had been pulled and lay in straight, tidy rows on each drill, ready to be snagged. Snagging, the removal of the leaves from the root, - took one of two forms, depending on the farmer's preference. The operation could either be executed by holding the root in one hand while skilfully severing the leaves and possibly a thin sliver of the crown, using a snagger or heavy knife, with the other hand. The alternative practice favoured by some beet growers was to use an instrument very much like a turf slane to chop off the foliage and hard crown, as the roots lay in rows after pulling. The former method seemed to be the most popular and always favoured in our household. If frost appeared likely during the beet pulling operation, the roots, instead of being left in rows on the drills as described above, were piled in heaps with the leaves of the outside layers draped downwards, thus helping to minimise frost damage. In this scenario, the knife "snagger" could be used without difficulty whereas the slane method was not an option.

The next two days and part of Saturday when Christy and I were able to join in, completed the snagging procedure. The beet crop now stood ready to be shifted to the collection point on the Killeigh road. Paddy Poland spent Monday morning trimming a whitethorn and privet hedge with a billhook and used the trimmings to reinforce the wheel tracks around the entrance gate to the beet field. The pulping action of the big cart wheels in the soft October earth, made this shoring-up necessary at the exit point through which all cart loads of beet had to pass. Tom Casey, who had to attend to some home chores that morning arrived just in time for his dinner of bacon and cabbage at one o' clock. As he tucked into the wholesome meal, mother fetched a winkers, a handful of oats in a tin basin, and hurried down to the Well field to "catch" the red mare, a relatively easy job. As soon as the mare heard the familiar rasping of the oat grains against the tin, she came galloping. A gentle pat on her white forehead, a little scratch underneath the chin and she paid far more attention to the contents of the basin than the feel of the winkers sliding over her ears or the bit into her mouth.

When Mother arrived back, Tom Casey, now waiting at the stable door, ceased manipulating the splinter of wheaten straw through his back molars, in a vain attempt to locate the offending nut of bacon rind and proceeded to yoke the mare. He slipped on the collar and hames, put a straddle on her back and fastened it underneath with the girth. He then placed the breechin' across the mare's haunches and backed her in underneath the cart with the red wheels, pulling down the shafts so that the backband chain slotted neatly into its groove on the straddle. He hooked the two draught chains on the cart to either side of the hames, the breechin' to the shafts and fastened the belly-band. Having secured the tail-board in position, Tom fitted the sideboards, threw two beet forks into the cart and drove away towards the beet field to commence shifting the beet to the collection point on the roadside. Waiting for him there he met his erstwhile team-mate Paddy Poland, who had by now completed his road repair work. Tom drove in, positioned the cart so as to leave a row of beet on either side, threw a beet fork to Paddy, spat on his hands and with a mild request for Divine assistance, muttered, "In the name of God, we'll make a start." The beet fork had six or seven prongs, each tipped with an oval or circular bead of metal, approximately half an inch in diameter. This design saved any damage to the root crop, which might otherwise result from the sharp points of an ordinary fork. Luckily, the beet collection point lay quite adjacent to the field so the removal operation was completed the following evening by working on for a while in the moonlight.

Next morning, the field where lush teeming leaves once rolled and waved in the breeze now looked bare and cheerless. Empty, save for the lines of withering stalks, soon to commence the cycle of returning to vegetable matter and thereby fertilise next year's crop of wheat, oats or barley. We now had the stage set for our beet harvest to be collected and taken away to the rail station at Tullamore for onward shipping to the sugar factory at Tuam. The final act of loading the beet into lorries at the collection point and then off-loading into a wagon at the rail station often proved to be the most arduous and punishing episode in the whole beet harvesting operation. Traditionally the weather at this time of the year was cold and wet. The farmer, of course, had to accompany the load from collection point to the rail head and might have to cycle the three, four or five miles in appalling weather conditions, unless the driver allowed him to throw his bicycle up on top of the load and give him a lift in the cab. Hail, rain or snow the beet then had to be off-loaded into the wagon with a beet fork. Several roots could fall between the wagon and the siding and these had to be collected by hand and thrown on to the load proper. All in all it was a difficult task getting the beet crop from the growing field to the rail station, for onward shipping to the Carlow or Tuam factory. However, weather conditions this year were good and the operation went without a hitch. Within a short while we would get news setting out technical information on the sugar content of the beet. With this in hand, the only outstanding facet remaining would be the postcard from the railway

Spring Grub
(Courtesy: Wexford County Library)

advising us that our allocation of beet pulp had arrived and lay ready for collection.

Beet pulp, the offal or residue of the root, after the sugar had been extracted always proved to be a popular and valuable supplement to all animal feed. It usually came in large, open mesh sacks for storage in the barn. The sacks, although long and cumbersome, were comparatively light. Consequently, at this time of the year the barn served as a favourite hiding place, in our many games of hide-and-seek. Who could ask for better fun than climbing over these wobbly, cushiony bags and sliding down between them, to find the almost perfect hiding place for any nine or ten year old.

Not all farmers in the locality sowed beet but that of course did not mean they were idle during October. Con Kelly, with his two graceful chestnut draught horses, during the past few days, had grubbed four acres of stubble, with his spring-grub and then used the same team to skin the bog field. Skinning expressed the term used for light ploughing, that is ploughing to a depth of no more than one and a half to two inches. After skinning, the field might be harrowed once or twice to separate the weeds and scutch grass from the soil, leaving them to wither and die. In certain extreme cases the weeds, roots and scutch were harrowed into rows, then using four-grained forks, the rows were manhandled into small piles and burned. Although back breaking work, it proved to be an effective way to clean out unwanted roots and like many other work procedures on the farm in those years could be described as very much environmentally friendly. Indeed, artificial weedkillers were almost unknown. The heaps of burning scutch-grass had a wonderful, tantalising aroma and I'm sure if the poets had been familiar with it they might have sung its praises just as high as they did when eulogising with nostalgia the smell of the peat fire from the thatched cottage.

Ned McEvoy had been busy with his grey pony drawing slabs or "slobs" as they were popularly called, from Muir's wood, to do some repair jobs on partitions and mangers in the outhouses. He later occupied himself cutting scollops, thin hazel rods used for basket making, cleeve or kish making and for thatching. Ned had arranged with local thatcher Fantin Kerwin to do his house before Christmas and nobody knew better than Ned, that the current days represented a good time to cut hazel scollops, when the leaves were gone and the sap down. Cleeves and kishes were large, rectangular basket-type containers, three feet wide, five feet long and one and a half feet deep. They were used with turf barrows when moving heaps of dry peat sods out from the soft turf bank to an access point, firm enough to accommodate the pony cart or donkey cart, when drawing home the turf. Indeed, in cases of emergency they were used to wheel a day's supply direct from the bog to the dwelling house.

In the hill field, which wanders down to the banks of

Cleeve or Kish (Courtesy: National Museum of Ireland, Dublin)

the Clodiagh at the rere of Kenna's cottage, the jangle of Joe
Condron's metal bound cart wheels, could be plainly heard as
they jolted over the gravel covered track, on the headland.
Joe endeavoured to beat the clock by drawing in the last few
loads of mangolds from this four acre field before darkness
fell. He had two men pulling and a youngster tidying the pit
in the haggard. Mangolds are very sensitive to frost so each
evening until the final load had been "heeled up" all hands
helped to cover the pit with a liberal thatch of old hay or
straw, topped off with shovelfuls of earth.

As evenings grew shorter and darkness set in earlier,
the young folk developed a greater interest in the October
Devotions. These devotions were conducted every Tuesday
and Friday evening during that month, in St. Patrick's church
in Killeigh and consisted of Rosary and Benediction for the
Holy Souls. On the surface it appeared the schoolgoers and
teenagers were devoutly supporting a worthy cause but on
deeper examination, the late devotions offered a marvellous

opportunity for the girls to meet the boys, or the boys to escort the girls home along the dark roadway after the prayer service. Indeed, with little or no organised amusement in country areas, such outings were a welcome break from the hum-drum days of school and many strenuous tasks on the farm. These were substantial reasons why week- evening religious ceremonies, missions and such like were well supported by schoolgoers and young adults, especially during the winter months. Even some parents admitted the outings were not without their plus side. It was not unknown for many of these friendships, built up during those carefree days, to mature and blossom into deeper commitment and eventual wedding bells. And in point of fact, for the newly marrieds to continue on attending the October Devotions for many years afterwards. The services culminated in special Halloween religious observances on the thirty first of October, with further solemnities on All Saints Day, the first of November. On All Souls' Day the second of November, another excuse to stay out after dark presented itself, because custom dictated, the more visits made to the Church the more souls were released from Purgatory.

However, more importantly for the young folk, Halloween was "Black face night" when the Pookas called. These were local lads, dressed up in tall hats, old trousers, jackets turned inside out, bright coloured scarves and faces blackened with burned cork or alternatively wearing vizards made with the help of brown cardboard and black boot polish. Travelling in groups of three or four they called on all houses in the locality and each played a musical instrument. Traditionally, the most favoured seemed to be the melodeon, mouth organ, tin whistle and badhran. The Pookas were always made to feel welcome. They performed their party piece on the kitchen floor, were clapped to the echo, got "thruppence" or sixpence from the woman of the house and then disappeared into the night, proceeding by bicycle, to their next engagement. Meeting these buckos on their mounts late at night, caused many an unsuspecting traveller to wonder if, after all, there were such things as ghosts or witches abroad on this spooky night. In some houses they were treated to a cup of tea and a helping of homemade cake or barm brack which contained thrupenny bits wrapped up in butter paper. Of course if the pookas were lucky enough to get the slice with the money, this added greatly to the hilarity and represented a welcome addition to their collection box.

With the pookas well and truly on their way the scene was set for some serious business in seasonal merriment. We put a lit candle inside the shell of a scooped out turnip and placed it in the front window. Mick had done a pretty good job on the sculpture, two slitty eyes, a small nose and wide mouth with what looked like genuine teeth, silhouetted against the candle light. The time honoured games of "sixpence in the basin" and "bite the apple" were the most popular.

"Ye'll get pneumonia dippin' yer heads in that frosty water", represented Mother's contribution as Christy, stripped to the shoulders, snorted and sneezed in his endeavours to lift the sixpenny piece in his teeth, from the bottom of the basin of water. After several attempts, he did at last succeed so another sixpence had to be found for the next challenger. This turned out to be a fruitless quest until older sister, Mary, solved the impasse by producing a thrupenny bit. Then Mick showed some dissent as he surfaced after three or four unsuccessful "dives."

"That's not fair, ye can't get a grip on it, it's much smaller than the sixpence", he protested.

"Well there's a penny," said Mother, as she threw one into the basin, "that should be big enough to get yer mouth around".

And so it was, Mick soon surfaced again with the brown penny between his teeth, and a smile from ear to ear.

"Bite the apple" turned out to be a little too boisterous. Several times we lost our grip as the apple swung out of control, suspended from a meat hook in the ceiling. On one orbit it miraculously missed smashing into the green, antique vase on the dresser. Luckily, Mother had gone out to get water from the pump and missed witnessing this near disaster. The vase was generations old, and we were so frightened, we collectively agreed to cut down the apple before some near miss became a reality. As a fair amount of energy had been used up we changed tactics, took out the playing cards and settled into a penny game of twenty fives using pennies, thrupenny bits and sixpences we had fished from the basin earlier.

Next morning Mother warned us if we were out in the fields, and were tempted to eat some of the last remaining blackberries, not to do so.

"Ye should never ate blackberries after Halloween", she warned, "the witches spit on them and after the first of November, they'd poison ye".

Well we took her word for it and as the morning wore on, stories filtered through of what the "good boys" or pookas had been up to the previous night. By tradition strange happenings occurred on Halloween night, pranks and practical jokes were common place and this year brought no exception. A wet sack had been thrown over Johnnie Dunne's

43

cottage chimney which of course forced the smoke back down into his kitchen. Poor Johnnie had to open his windows for a while then quench the fire and go off to bed early. Some renegade had spun around the fingerboard at Gorteen bridge to give wrong directions to unsuspecting travellers. Mike Cooke's iron gate was lifted off its hinges and thrown into his haggard. Last year the shafts of his donkey cart were rammed through the gate and the donkey yoked to it, from the other side. Although the jokes were an imposition on the people at the receiving end, nevertheless, they accepted them in good part and with a certain air of inevitability.

3   Goin' to Grannie's

The extended Halloween merrymaking ushered in November, the first month of winter, with its murky mists and patchy fogs which hung like scattered wisps of sheep wool across the moors. The irregular layers of fog also wafted and drifted along the low-lying areas between Hawkswood and Derrybeg on the Tullamore road. They posed an extra hazard in the dark evenings for cyclists who for one reason or another tarried too long in town, not realising they had left their carbide lamps at home.

"Curse a blazes," growled Martin Dunne, as he tried to steer a half dozen calves into his haggard. "I wouldn't mind if it was one thing or dother; if 'twas all fog, ye could handle it, but runnin' in an out o' these bloody patches, ye never know whether ye have all the calves or not."

However, as it's only early days yet let's not be too hard on November, the ninth month of the old Roman calendar when the chestnut, sycamore, oak and beech present themselves as "Indian Princes before they turn to ghosts". When new catkins hang like Chinese lanterns from the hazel and alder and hedgerows yield up their wide variety of berries to the sparrow, finch and wren. When on clear days a lovely Autumn scent of dead bracken and fallen leaves permeates the crisp dry air.

After lengthy negotiations and much diplomacy Mother again succeeded in arranging the services of Paddy Poland and our uncle Tom Casey to commence pulling the turnip crop in the inner moor. This time, Paddy and Tom were both armed with a turnip snagger, a broad , sturdy, reasonably sharp, short handled knife, replicas of which were oft' times hammered out by George Plunkett, the local blacksmith, from the head of a broken billhook or briar hook. The snagger had a twofold purpose in the turnip pulling operation. It removed the excess soil from the turnip after pulling and then chopped away the stalk or crown, taking the leaves with it, in one swift stroke. The leaves were thrown in one alley and the turnips in the one beside it. This arrangement simplified the subsequent loading operation with a beet fork. The amazing dexterity displayed by turnip pullers, in the use of this knife, had to be seen to be believed. It took literally seconds to pull the root, knock off the excess clay with two or three downward strokes, then holding the turnip over the intended furrow or drill, administer the coup-de-gras which detached it from the stalk and leaves.

Tom and Paddy worked hard for two days, then Christy and I joined in on Saturday. Even if they could use them there were no spare "snaggers" for junior brothers Mick and Tim. Anyway, mother insisted "they're far too young to be handlin' snaggin' knives, d' ye want them to chop off two or three fingers, tryin' to keep up with the min?" Of course we were delighted to be the big fellas, and dressing up in well worn jackets, scarves and the inevitable jute bag leggings added that extra touch of glamour. We had helped pulling mangolds and turnips last year and could not be classified as amateurs. Indeed we only lost a few yards on the men as we came to the end of each drill and they always helped us to finish out.

No matter what field job was in progress on the farm, eleven o' clock "tay" on the headland was a must. By ten thirty the strain on our constantly bent backs began to tell. Shortly afterwards, we were delighted to see Mary arrive on the headland weighed down with the usual old tattered brown shopping bag in one hand and a "gallon" of "tay" in the other. Gallon in this case did not mean a measure, it signified the name of the utensil in which the "tay" was being carried. This bright tin container, two or three of which we had purchased from the tinkers on their most recent visit to the area, was always referred to as a gallon. Every household kept a few for various uses like milking cows, holding buttermilk, bringing drinking water to the bog, hayfield or cornfield and last but by no means least, for bringing eleven o' clock or four o' clock "tay" to the turnip-field. There is no doubt of course, that the vessel originally got its name from its cubic capacity. Not thinking too much then about how the item got its name we all plodded towards the sheltered headland, picked out the section of ditch with most shelter and least briars and sat down. The broad, high hedges which separated farmers' fields were locally referred to as "ditches."

Paddy Poland immediately took charge of the gallon, removed the lid and poured out piping hot "tay" into the four blue and white striped mugs, which he had taken from the tattered bag. Mary smartly produced a neatly wrapped brown paper parcel, opened it and handed round to each member of the team two slices of brown homemade bread, "buttered" with marmalade and butter. The gang certainly welcomed the break and yarns were swapped as we pulled each other's leg, while all the time doing justice to the "elevenses" and throwing the odd crust to the most daring sparrow or greenfinch.

"Ye can see the sheeaun, Colton's fairy fort, very plainly from here", said Tom as he cleared his throat and lit one of his favourite Woodbines. "Ye wouldn't want to be passin' that place on a dark November evenin'," he

Turnip Pulper.

continued, looking towards Paddy with a glint in his eye and hoping Christy and I were taking it all in. "I believe two banshees come out every evening in November to comb their hair. If ye passed near them they'd throw their comb at ye, an' if it hit ye, ye'd be dead before mornin' ."

"Aye, bedad! that's a fact," nodded Paddy, "bein' small she has a better chance o' hittin' a gossoon with the comb than a grown man."

We couldn't grasp that logic so I asked Paddy how it could be easier to hit something small than something big. Of course Paddy had the answer. "Sure the banshee is only a foot high, and she could hit someone her own size much easier than a bigger person like me or yer uncle Tom."

Although we didn't believe the story and took it all with a grain of salt, still we would never dream of going near Colton's sheeaun in the dark. In fact, if the situation arose we'd pass by fairly smartly in broad daylight. I told Paddy that earlier in the year, I had written out four or five folklore stories which Mr. Hutton our teacher passed on to The Irish Folklore Commission Survey and one of them concerned Colton's sheeaun. I pointed out that Mr. Hutton, who knew a lot about this fairy fort read my story carefully and never mentioned anything about the banshee. However, this didn't sway Paddy, he just passed me off saying, "Ah, sure he didn't want to frighten one of his good pupils."

That Saturday evening completed the pulling of the turnips and the following week, when neither uncle Mike or uncle Tom were available, Paddy finished the job by drawing them all in and pitting them in the shelter of the larch trees at the upper end of the haggard.

The hob-nail boots which we got after the threshing are now serving us well on our daily trips to and from Killurin school. However, for the time being Mother insists we take them off and change into our old ones before starting the evening chores, - pulping turnips, putting hay in the mangers and cleaning out stables. With the approach of chilly weather, the cows, calves and horses are now housed at night time. Interestingly, farmers' ploughing and tilling teams were always referred to as horses whether male or female. Our own gentle animals were in fact mares but nevertheless we used the expressions, as did every other farmer, "yoke the horses," "feed the horses" or "give hay to the horses."

On our way home from school a gang of us as we often did before, climbed the iron gate into Dooley's turnip field and pilfered a large purple swede. We proceeded to smash it into pieces against the sharp corner of the stone pier and distributed the tasty segments to the waiting hands. Some of the more adventurous of the girls joined in and that meant we had to organise a second raid on the turnip field to make up for the extra demand. By the time we arrived home and despite our aperitif in raw turnips, we still suffered from pangs of that rare hunger that's known only to schoolboys.

While we slipped off our new foot gear and

Hay knife.

exchanged them for a pair of black "wellies," our mother had taken the large metal pan of fried potatoes and cabbage from the bed of cinders on the hob and set out our portions on warm plates on the newly scrubbed wooden table, each with a mugful of fresh milk. It didn't take long to clear the plates but as always there were a few spare potatoes available in the black skillet pot, in which they were cooked. The pot was usually left hanging to one side on the crane and it hung there from normal dinner time at one o' clock, until the schoolgoers arrived home at three thirty or four p.m. These spares were tasty and hot with enticing brown baked roasted skins. Having helped ourselves to a few of our choice, covered in butter, and with tummies full we moved off to commence "fodderin' " the animals.

Mick took charge of the pulper and mashed many piles of turnips and mangolds which he then shovelled into galvanised iron buckets, topping off each bucket with a handful of bran, cracked oats or beetpulp, depending on the animal being fed. He dispensed the rations into the wooden troughs of every manger, whether for cow, calf or horse. In the meantime, Christy sharpened that practical tool, the hay knife, with its twin handles and broad edged blade. As I watched him struggling with the broken half of a sharpening stone I could only reflect on the ingenuity of uncle Mike and his frame-mounted grinding stone. It was ingeniously driven by a bicycle chain and two bicycle gear wheels. So simple, so effective, operated by foot pedal, thus leaving his arms free to hold the instrument being sharpened. Christy mounted the old wooden ladder lying against the rick, removed the canvas cover and with slow downward strokes, neatly cut a new bench of sweet smelling hay to a depth of nine or ten inches. Then with his two-grain fork, lifted a few layers and turned them over the edge to the ground below. He proceeded to distribute the forkfuls to each intended manger and by the time he finished, his jacket and cap looked as if they had collected sufficient quantities of Italian ryegrass and clover seeds to sow a new meadow.

I, being the eldest, usually got the dirty job of cleaning out the cow house, calf shed and stables; wheeling the manure on to the dung heap with a boxbarrow and then putting fresh, dry straw on the floors for the animals to lie on at night. These were everyday jobs, they had to be performed each evening after school and at some time during the day on Saturdays and Sundays depending on the timing of the hurling match in Kellys' field.

Mike and Tom Casey had now spent a substantial amount of time with us since the threshing. Our own crops of beet, turnips, mangolds and potatoes were safely harvested, so Mother suggested, "a couple o' you lads should go down to Killeenmore every Saturday for the next few weeks and help out yer uncles with milkin', fodderin' and general yard work. They'll want to be puttin' out manure on the stubbles, and drawin' bog stuff for that ould grazin' field at Gallaghers."

Bog stuff, taken in cart loads from the low bank on the bog could be described as the forerunner of modern day

Dash churn.

peat moss. Heavier, darker and more moist but highly beneficial in keeping down moss and promoting grass growth both in meadow and pasture land.

"Goin' to Grannie's," was how we described going to Killeenmore. Although a kindly lady, with her snow white hair rolled into a neat ball at the back of her head and a big blue apron, Grannie could often be very strict. Nevertheless, we loved her and her chunky, homemade marmalade. The same couldn't be said about her butter with the very strong tang which she, herself produced in a dash churn.

"Ye don't get proper butter from them ould tumble churns, like yer mother has Tommie, ye need the dash churn to get the right flavour," she'd say, handing me a slice of soda bread adorned with a copious cover of her own butter and topped off with tasty segments of marmalade. Were it not for the marmalade I'd never manage to eat the slice. As things worked out, I was the only one who could travel to Killeenmore on the first week-end. Cycling through Killeigh village and down Graigue hill on the Friday evening astride my small framed Raleigh bicycle, I felt proud about the bicycle because I bought it for one pound ten shillings with money hard earned while working at various jobs for neighbours. I always looked forward to visiting Grannie's. I had my own bed in the upstairs room in which uncle Mike slept, much better than home where I had to share a bed with my brothers. My uncle Ned loved sessions with the tin whistle and fiddle while Mike preferred to play the melodeon or flute. This time he seemed anxious to teach me the basic steps in ceili dancing, "The siege of Ennis," "The bridge of Athlone," and "The waves of Tory" were his favourites.

Taking down the melodeon proved to be the cue for Grannie to run the twig over the large square and oblong flags of the stone floor, finishing off the job with a besom, a neatly tied bunch of long stemmed bog heather to shift the remaining dust from the crevices between each flagstone. After some initial floundering, getting both my feet in each other's way, Mike jumped on to the floor light as a feather. "Look," says he, "there's nothin' to it, one two three, one two three, one two three four five six seven, one two three, - try it agin."

I had another go and showing some improvement, earned a further ten minutes coaching. Although the progress seemed steady I got the feeling that Mike had had enough for this lesson because he drifted off into a medley of his favourite ballads, "The wearin' of the green," "Kelly from Killane," and "Boulevogue."

"We'll give it a go some other night" he suggested, "and in the manetime, you do a bit o' practice."

Grannie had gone off to bed earlier so it fell to us to brew up a cup of tea and reduce her store of ginger nuts. Tea finished, Mike sent me scurrying up the stairs with the warning, "It's a bit late for you to be hangin' around the fire, I'll be draggin' you out at seven o'clock in the mornin'." He then went out to check on some animals in the outhouses before locking up for the night.

Saturday the last Saturday in November dawned crisp, cool and dry. I didn't get "dragged out at seven" as my uncle had threatened, but hopped out of my own accord, at half past seven. Mike's bed looked tossed and empty, he obviously had wakened before his little alarm clock rang and succeeded in dressing himself without disturbing me. The tiny alarm clock with its yellow stained dial, no larger than a half-crown in diameter, appeared to be one of Mike's prized possessions.

"I bought it on a fair day, twenty years ago, for two and sixpence, and it never lost a minute," he boasted.

"An' how could it lose a minute?" quipped Grannie, with a twinkle in her eye, "when there's no minute hand on it since you broke the glass, with a flash lamp, that night a couple o' years ago."

No matter who rose early, nobody got up before Grannie. She had been rattling pots and pans since half past six and had produced for us a big "burner" of wholemeal stirabout, followed by a warm breakfast of fried eggs and sausages. My agenda for the day was to accompany Mike on a long overdue fencing job on the boundary line between his two grazing moors and the bog wood. Some of his yearling bullocks were consistently breaking out to sample the green grazing along the bog road, where several "joults" were filled last spring with scutch grass. In the meantime the scutch had grown, and now appeared as a tasty morsel in comparison to the scarce croppings on the moor. Mike of course worried if the cattle wandered too far one might very easily finish up in a bog drain.

The fencing equipment, barbed wire, oak stakes,

sledgehammer, crowbar, hammer and staples were loaded into the horse cart and sitting on the slat with legs dangling we jogged off to our destination. As the day wore on I had a feeling my uncle seemed delighted with the help.

"For a twelve year old, ye're fairly handy with the crowbar," he admitted and I didn't bother to disagree and tell him I was only eleven years and eight months. Anyway, he asked me to swap jobs and hammer in a few staples. "A change is as good as a rest," he continued and I readily agreed. I had made so many stake holes with the crowbar, my arm muscles were feeling heavy and rigid. I felt a little "done in" after this Saturday stint in Killeenmore. I always seemed to work harder there than I did at home. Maybe it became a question of pride, trying to be just as good as grown men. I now wondered if I might be too stiff to put in a good performance tomorrow, at right full back for the Killeigh juvenile hurling team against arch rivals, Killoughy. Although Grannie wanted me to stay on until Sunday morning I decided to set out for home after tea, but not before I assured her I had a good flashlamp in working order and that I had no fears about cycling at night time.

Graigue hill was too steep to cycle up on the way home, although the hardest part of the incline covered no more than eighty or ninety yards of road. The bare limbs of the beech, oak and whitethorn which grew on either side had long since intertwined overhead, producing a tunnel effect, especially when covered in the rich foliage of summer-time. As I dismounted, the wind moaning through the creaking branches rustled the few remaining leaves on the beech and created in me a strange feeling of isolation. Just then I remembered I had heard stories from my mother about farmers in Newtown and Killeenmore, who had seen ghosts near Graigue hill, on certain nights during the winter. My steps quickened and I even felt a little assured in having a bicycle with me for company. The speeded up clatter of the steel tips on the heels of my boots echoed against the hard dry road and distinctly gave the impression of a second pair of feet following. In a cold sweat, I mustered up enough strength in my legs to run the remainder of the sixty yard stretch until I got out from under the menacing branches, and could see the welcome light from the paraffin lamp in Conroy's cottage window. At that point I somehow experienced a surge of renewed energy, mounted the bicycle and laboriously pumped the pedals to the top of the climb.

It was now all downhill to Killeigh village and then level ground for the remainder of the journey. A great feeling like one reprieved from the gallows engulfed me as I sang and whistled into the night, no longer feeling any aches or pains in the muscles which had absorbed so much strain during the day. I became immersed in an all-consuming sense of joie-de-vivre and vowed never again to walk Graigue hill on my own on a winter's night.

4   Christmas

The year's clock ticked steadily onwards and now had both hands firmly pointing to twelve, December, the last month of the year. We all looked forward so much to December and Christmas. Perhaps, this year Santy might pay us a visit or at least pay a visit to the three youngest, Mick, Margaret and Tim. I was now little more than eleven and a half years old; Mary, the eldest, thirteen and five months, Christy, nine and a half and so on downwards in one and a half or two year gaps to Timothy who boasted five and a half years. When I was seven and a half our Dad died leaving Mother with six children aged between one and a half and nine years. I'm sure she had more heartbreaking moments than us in years when Santy failed to arrive. She found it so extremely difficult to make ends meet that having clothes and food at Christmas for six young ones, as well as herself, represented a supreme achievement without thinking of presents. However, there were exceptions to the case. Santy did bring books, dolls, steamrollers and fire engines in other years and we had a few very thoughtful neighbours who, on occasions, gave Santy a helping hand with cap-guns, coloured balls and writing cases.

With darkness now descending shortly after four o' clock in the evenings activity grew less and less out on the farms, even in good weather. John Corbett, Jimmie Gibson and other big tillage men who grew substantial acreage of beet were carting out farmyard manure on to stubble fields to have it ploughed in before Christmas and decomposing to enrich the soil for next year's crop. Joe Fletcher and some of the other locals cut and breasted the few remaining ditches they failed to complete in November. The cuttings, branches and roots were piled in gangly heaps and always reminded me of great magpies nests. They were left for ten or twelve days to lose further sap, and then burned. We loved the smell of burning bushes and enjoyed the thrill of chasing each other through the spirals of blue and white smoke, that wafted out from these piles of blackthorn, sedge and briar. Awkward questions had to be answered of course, when we arrived home, as to how in Heaven's name we got "that horrible smell on our good school ganseys."

Activities around our own home now concentrated on the count-down to Christmas. Mother whitewashed all walls of the dwelling house both inside and outside. This apparently remained a special job reserved for her alone, we were never allowed to take the whitewashing brush in hand except for the outhouses and stable. When eventually, like a landscape painter, she had applied the final touches to the last

Well kept thatched house with white-washed walls in Killeigh Parish.(Courtesy: John Kearney, Offaly Historical and Archaeological Society, Tullamore)

remaining kitchen wall she handed the gear over to myself and Christy, but not without first directing us to the areas she considered priorities.

"Ye can start on the front wall and the two front piers, then work yer way across to the outhouses. Be careful ye don't get splatters o' lime in yer eyes, and don't let anything happen to that new brush."

We had already dressed ourselves up in our "turnip pulling apparel" complete with old overcoat tied with binder twine and wide brimmed scarecrow hats to save our faces from the lime. To us this whitewashing job represented a bit of diversion. We had no fine lines to adhere to on the rough stone walls of the outhouses and even the preparation of the mixture - boiling water and lime in a bucket with a pinch of blue added - presented no problems. It was fun to watch the white, lava-like bubbles swell and burst as we splashed the boiling water into the lime and stirred the mixture with a pot-stick. The whitewashing brush too proved easy to handle. The broad head with pliable bristle fibres ensured that the minimum of effort covered large areas. Taking turns, we completed in just five evenings, the internal and external work on all the outhouses which needed whitewashing, including the three partitions in the cow-house and the single partition in the stable. We even found time, on occasions, to daub some smart graffiti on each other's back while the unsuspecting one laboured on, deeply engrossed in preparation work like wire-brushing a wall or cleaning down a manger.

With the annual decorating jobs now complete we turn our attentions, each evening to more menial and arduous tasks. These included filling pot-holes in the back and front yards with shovelfuls of river gravel, trimming grass margins and sawing sufficient firewood to see us well through the Christmas season.   Then the dirtiest job of all, we had to clean the soot from the kitchen chimney using a carefully selected cone-shaped holly bush tied to a long hazel pole. This contraption when pushed up and down vigorously in a twisting motion did the job most effectively.   On occasions the soot might be stored in sacks for eventual use on vegetable and onion ridges. We obtained the raw material for firewood from oak, beech or sycamore branches blown down in spring and autumn storms or from young birch which grew in abundance on the bog. We first of all cut the branches into workable dimensions, then using a trestle and crosscut, sawed the lengths into ten inch logs. Logs too large in diameter for easy handling were split into three or four pieces with a hatchet. In some tough cases, when confronted with knotted chunks, we called on the services of a sledgehammer and an iron wedge.   The work was hard and strenuous especially using the crosscut with the monotonous, non-stop, forward and backward motion of the arms, we naturally ran

Crosscut.

out of breath and often had to stop for short breaks. As was the case with many young lads in those days an element of rivalry reared its head in almost every job we did. On occasions, neither would give in to stop sawing until an unrelenting pain in the arms allowed no further movement. These extra tasks, in preparation for the coming festivities, were of course over and above our normal daily assignments. The "fodderin' " had to be done every evening without fail and now in mid December, much of it had to be attended to with the aid of a stable-lamp, the forerunner of what today might be termed a storm-lantern. This marvellous sturdy paraffin lamp with its squat durable globe neatly nesting inside a bright robust wire guard, was an absolute must in every farmyard during the winter months. Indeed, in our household, as soon as normal evening tasks were complete we had to take it in turn to "carry the lamp." This meant carrying, holding and taking full charge of the stable-lamp while our mother milked the cows, strained the milk in the outside milk parlour and apportioned the quantity which would go to the cream crock, for eventual churning, and the quantity to be allotted to household requirements.

It sounds deceptively simple, but we found carryin' the lamp had inbuilt hazards which were numerous and varied. Many a time and oft' the flame blew out on windy nights and no doubt most of these windy nights were also wet and cold. The carrier then had to feel his way in the dark, through the howling gale, back to the kitchen fireplace and re-light it. The chances were reasonably high that the flame blew out again on the return trip, then the procedure had to be repeated. Expecting sympathy from any brothers or sisters sitting in the warmth of the kitchen was a nonstarter. Indeed, very often, experience proved it to be the reverse.

"Put the lamp in a bucket an' it won't blow out," one of them jeered, while the rest laughed in accord.

Foolish enough to take this advice on one occasion, I found with the lamp in the bucket I had no light to see where I was walking and finished up floundering in puddles of rainwater. On arrival at the cowshed, the greeting from Mother went something like this:- "What kept ye,? leavin' me sittin' here like Kitty the Hare with no light. I tried to carry on but more milk went on the ground than into the gallon."

Then of course we had problems with our polly cow, a kicker and a tail-flicker. On more than one winter's night she managed to swish that tail, just at the opportune moment to either knock the lamp out of our hand, knock off the globe or even smash the globe with the power of the flick. On another occasion we had an incident where the little Kerry Blue cow, with the sore udder, or "paps" as Mother called them, danced to one side, put her back left foot into the milk gallon and then managed to walk on the carrier's foot. Luckily, he succeeded in maintaining his balance, remained in an upright position and real pandemonium was averted.

On windy nights such as these but when clouds were firm and no rain falling, we knew that robins, blackbirds, thrushes and chaffinches roosted on the low branches of trees and bushes along the most sheltered ditches. One such ditch stretched across the south end of the "first field," and this ditch gained further shelter from the tall trees growing around that small square patch, we called the "new garden." We understood why the first field got its name, being the nearest field to the dwelling house but why the "new garden" basked in such an up-to-date title, we had no idea. It must have been a later addition to the farm than the orchard which

gloried in the more ancient terminology, the "ould garden."
After tea we might dress up in top-coat, scarf and cap, arm
ourselves with a flashlamp or carbide lamp and battle the
sou' wester across the first field to the high ditch, which
formed the north boundary of the new garden. We loved
doing this to count the birds and like the log cutting sessions
with the crosscut, there had to be an element of rivalry.

"I counted thirteen blackbirds and eight robins,"
boasted Christy.

"Ah! hard luck," said Mick, "I got fifteen blackbirds
and nine robins."

Then the inevitable disputes.

"You got fifteen because you included four of mine,"
countered Christy, "and that means you only found eleven
blackbirds yourself."

However, with a cold wind blowing the squabbles
didn't turn out to be too serious, and by the time we got back
to the warmth of the kitchen fire, there was more interest
displayed in a plate of stirabout, before bed-time, than in
pursuing arguments concerning the number of birds listed.

It's now the eighteenth of December, only a week to
go until the twenty fifth. Excitement is growing daily as we
make preparations to commence our special Christmas
assignments. In recent weeks while cutting firewood we
spared a thick, two-pronged, vee-shaped section of beech
tree, with yule logs in mind for the Christmas fires. Now
armed with a re-vamped crosscut we set about sawing this
smooth-barked beauty and after much exertion and many
rests converted it into three chunky logs, sufficient to cover
that special fire on Christmas eve, Christmas day and St.
Stephen's day. Procuring the yule log was very much part
and parcel of the preparations in many households and

certainly was the case in ours. When cut, the logs were left out in the open air to the mercy of the elements. If stored indoors, even for six or seven days, they tended to dry out and lose sap, resulting in a shorter fire life. This could not be countenanced because of course, the longer the fire life the greater the enjoyment.

It would be unthinkable to have to visit a potato pit for household needs on any of the twelve days of Christmas, so our next priority had to be the sorting of three or four "butts o' spuds" which we loaded into a boxbarrow and then wheeled them, one by one, into the barn situated reasonably close to the dwelling house. An element of fun crept into this chore because we took turns getting "jants" in the barrow on the return trips. As boys will be boys, a little hazard and adventure had to be added. This could take the form of simply racing the passenger as fast as possible down the hill behind the barn, then bringing the barrow to a sudden halt by ramming it head-on into the side of a straw rick. Absolute enjoyment, both for the driver and the passenger and occasioned many many happy moments of hearty laughter. Good clean fun you might say but with a gang of lads, the fun could never end without its share of devilment. Pushing the barrow with its unfortunate passenger on board, as far as possible into the duck pond and leaving it there, was a favourite gimmick, while the driver laughed and jeered from the comparative safety of dry ground. Wheeling it into a muddy puddle, then tilting it to one side until the hitch-hiker, with loud protestations, either scrambled out or fell out, was another ploy. If he fell out, then the laugh was greater but of course so was the trouble the driver garnered for adding further washboard scrubbing time to the duties of an already overworked mother. With the seasonal needs in eating potatoes now nicely sorted and stored, the procedure was repeated the following evenings, handling turnips and mangolds for animal feeding. These stocks, to cover three or four days, were deposited in the pulper house and not touched until Christmas eve. Rations for the intervening days were taken in directly from the pits and pulped there and then. Of course the wheelbarrow escapades persisted for the duration of this work, but possibly in a more subdued manner.

Our thoughts now turned to our next concern, procuring an ample supply of good green holly with no rusty leaves and a generous adornment of red berries. Weeks earlier suitable bushes were earmarked in the furry field along the ditch "mearnin' " Fletcher's and Purcell's bog. On Saturday we took an old Bushman saw and a billhook and set out on the holly trail. The billhook was used to clear away briars and white-thorn "sceachs" at the base of the tree, thus giving easier access to the holly branches. This instrument was never used to cut the holly because any strike against a limb might dislodge several ripe, red berries. We cut with the Bushman instead, sawing off one or two medium-sized shoots, carefully chosen for their abundance of sprays and berries. Some years had elapsed since we previously used this particular tree for our holly supply and it would now be given a few more free seasons, to accommodate the growth of new shoots. Mike Casey had advised us for conservation reasons, although I'm sure he never heard that word, to cut a different bush each year. This posed no problem for us, there were alternative prolific nests of holly trees available in the long field, in Clooney's field and down Poland's lane. In fact, last year we did procure our supply in Poland's lane and as a bonus, had the good fortune to ferret out and cut the makings of a very fine blackthorn stick, with a nicely proportioned knob for a handle. I well remember on our way home, seeing Paddy Poland standing at his hall door.

"Be japers! ye got a blackthorn as well as the holly, lads," said Paddy.

"We did indeed," we agreed, "Grandad is always looking for good walking sticks."

"D'ye know the best time of the year to cut a blackthorn?," continued Paddy, with what we considered a reprimanding tone in his voice. Feeling slightly guilty, it flashed through our minds we might have done wrong by cutting the young sapling at this time.

"No, when's the best time to cut one?," ventured Christy.

"When ye see one," said Paddy, with a glint of devilment in his eye as he burst into one of his loud, hearty laughs. "The best time to cut a blackthorn stick is when ye see one," repeated Paddy again, retrieving his equilibrium.

With most of these special assignments now behind us, and with only three or four days to Christmas eve, our work schedule appeared to be more or less up to date. We therefore put in strong pleas to be allowed go to Tullamore with Mother to help with the shopping. Spare money was a rarity in our household, but if at all possible a special effort was made to hold back the sale of bonhams, a young heifer or a calf for the December market, in order to have some ready cash for Christmas needs. This of course might not always be feasible and in the years with no stock for sale, Santy either passed by or forgot our address. However, this year thank heavens, we sold three young bull calves, one a white head, in the November fair and most of that money had been put by for this special occasion. The frustration of the lean years weighed much heavier on our mother than it did on us. No doubt she felt many heart pangs watching our eager faces while not being able to afford the little things she'd like to buy for all of us especially at Christmas time.

As luck would have it we discovered after some wheeling and dealing that myself and Mick were next in turn to go to town. Following an early breakfast of home made brown bread and butter with a mugful of tea, we yoked Kerry the red pony to his little blue shafted cart, the floor of which had already been lined with a bundle of fresh oaten straw. Then covering the sitting board with a well worn fibre cushion, we placed it in position across the cart, tied Kerry to the front gate, giving him a handful of hay to keep him occupied until Mother had sorted out her wares. She didn't delay very long. Kerry had scarcely munched his first wisp when she stepped sprightly through the front door carrying two brown baskets, both containing four dozen fresh eggs, and each egg individually wrapped in a page of some out-dated issue of "Irelands' Own." At this time of year demand was reasonably brisk, so the eight dozen at one and

Cart with Creels.
(Courtesy: Derryglad Folk Museum, Curraghboy, Athlone)

ninepence per dozen should fetch fourteen shillings, sufficient to pay for sundry items like tea, sugar, lard, Christmas candles and paraffin oil.

By stepping on to the base of an upturned wooden tub Mother eased herself on to the sitting board while we untied the pony, placed the unused hay in the cart for later, opened the gate and handed her the reins. Then, acting the big fellas, we placed one foot on a red wooden spoke of the cart wheel and swung our bodies on to the straw floor.

"How many times have I told you buckos not to do that?" she shouted, "if the pony moved forward ye could finish up with two broken legs, Why didn't ye use the tub like I did?"

All was silent in the back of the cart until I ventured, "Alright Mammy! we won't do it again."

"Hmm", she said, "how many times have I heard that before? ye won't do it agin 'til the next time." With a flick of the reins and a crisply spoken, "Giddy up, Kerry," we were on our way in a sling trot to Gorteen bridge, which spans the Clodiagh river. There we swung right, on to the Tullamore road.

In situations like this, Mother kept a stern face especially since she had to give us a tongue lashing for mounting the cart by way of the wheel spokes. Mick and I did not venture to ask any questions, we carried on our own conversation such as it was, until she eventually broke the ice.

"I suppose neither of you lads have a brass farthin' between ye?"

I knew Mick only had one shilling but I had saved four shillings and sixpence since helping Freddie Colton with some farm work in October. I briefly outlined our financial standing, and her only comment was to the effect, "she would see what she could do for Mick". Nestling down in the straw, with peaked caps pulled low over our foreheads, hand-knitted navy blue woollen scarves wound tightly about our necks and tucked deeply inside the inevitable brown ganseys, we were conscious of the bite in the cold, dry December air. Kerry trotted steadily on along the hard road through Scrubb, Derrybeg and Cloncon, past hedgerows looking bare and gaunt in their winter garb. We had little or no heat from the pale diluted sun as it struggled to make intermittent appearances low in the south eastern sky.

A great air of business pervaded the market square as we slowly made our way through haggling groups of buyers and sellers. All shapes and colours of donkey carts, pony carts and horses' carts, with wisps of straw sticking out through red or blue creels, crammed the area. Farmers filling their pipes and doing deals, farmers' wives trimming their baskets, but all keeping a keen eye on their clutches of pink skinned bonhams, so well washed that their little white bristles shone like silver. Others policing their plump geese, well fed chickens, suck calves, fresh vegetables, sacks of good eating potatoes, loads of fire logs or best quality black turf. Ninety per cent of all stock and produce, to the mutual benefit of buyer and seller, would change hands before the end of the day.

We had scarcely dismounted from the cart when the manager of a small local hotel approached, asking if the baskets contained eggs or country butter. When Mother advised him the contents, he took the complete lot at her budgeted price of fourteen shillings for the eight dozen. While the sale was in progress, I tied Kerry to a lamp standard and gave him the remainder of the hay we brought with us. Nearby, I tuned into a fascinating bargain between a pig dealer and Tim Hennessey, a neighbour of ours who had eight ten- week old bonhams for sale. Tim was holding out for twenty six shillings each. The dealer had offered nineteen shillings, pointing out that "the sucks weren't all that big for ten weeks," and walked away. Shortly afterwards, Tim called him back, "I'll tell ye what! ye can have the six big ones for twenty five shillings, and the two smaller ones for twenty two."

"Curse a blazes," said the dealer, "there's none o' them worth twenty five shillings."

"Now don't be actin' the maggot," said Tim, "I know bloody well you paid twenty four shillings last month, for four ruts ye bought off Mrs. Conroy."

"Ruts be damned", countered the dealer, "they were twice the size o' yours."

Just then another neighbour, Ned "The Duck" Mullally, who obviously had overheard part of the discussion arrived on the scene.

"Nice clutch o' sucks," says he, "God bless them, what's between ye?".

"Ah! it's not as simple or as azey as that", said the dealer, "it's a bit complicated, he's lookin' for two different prices, one for the ruts and another for the rest o' them."

"Forget about the two prices, Tim", said "The Duck", "what's yer bottom price for the eight?."

"I wouldn't sell them for a penny less than twenty three shillings," said Tim.

"Ah! that's not yer bottom," said "The Duck", catching Tim by the arm, "what is yer bottom? twenty two?"

"Bedad it's not," said Tim, "but if ye twist me arm like that, I might go to twenty two and sixpence."

"Now what's yer best offer?" he said to the dealer, "an' I mean yer best."

"They're not worth a penny more than twenty shillings and sixpence to me," said the dealer, "an' if he's here all day he won't even get that money from anyone else."

"Twenty shillings an' sixpence sounds too much like a fraction," said "The Duck", "an' sure no one understands fractions, make it twenty one shillings."
The dealer looked at the ground and didn't reply, "The Duck" concluded this gesture meant he was in agreement.

"Now there's only one and sixpence between ye and Tim has come down by four shillings while you ony raised yer offer by two. If Tim comes down another sixpence an' you go up a bob, ye can have the sucks at twenty two shillings aich."
After an anxious moment of silence, Tim spat on his hand, held it out and muttered, "It's a dale."
The dealer hesitated, looked at "The Duck" then spat on his hand and slapped it down on Tim's outstretched palm! The deal was done!

Obviously our mother had become as much interested in the proceedings as we were, she made no effort to move until the agreement became mutual.

"The buyer got a fair bargain there," she mused, "Tim always had good sucks," then with more urgency in the tone, "come on you pair and let's get the pony down to Rhattigan's yard, or we'll be here all day."

Rhattigans was a general grocery store and in common with many other similar stores of that time, had a fine back yard to accommodate the country folks with their carts and traps. As a convenience, they also stocked many items of light hardware - mousetraps, brush handles, Sacred

Heart lamps, candles and such like. Although there were many occasions throughout the year when the necessity arose for us to purchase goods on credit or had them "put in the book", we were nevertheless rated as a reasonably good customer.

On arrival, the shop-boy greeted us with a warm, "Good morning Mrs. Murray, and a very happy Christmas to you and yours; two fine big lads ye have there, so what can I do for you this time?'

As she handed him a prepared list Mother suitably replied for us all.

"Many happy returns to you Jimmie, and thanks for puttin' up with me during the year".

Jimmie glanced at the first item on the list, six pounds of sugar. Then taking a bright metal scoop from the open sack at the end of the counter, proceeded to fill three small, black paper sugar bags. He tapped the bottoms against the well worn but smooth oak counter to level off the contents and with expert movements of thumb and fingers, neatly folded and securely closed the tops of the bags. Each pack felt so firm it could be held upside down without fear of spilling a single grain of sugar. In our local shop at home, Mrs. Carolan never mastered these packing skills, instead she roughly closed down the top and tied the bag with white tea twine. To us, her system appeared almost an art in its own right. The raw material, a ball of light twine was kept on the counter in a red tin box with a hole in the arched lid, through which the twine was fed. It was no ordinary box. Mounted on one corner it had a small cutting knife with a partially concealed blade. After tieing the pack she held it above the knife, then with a firm downward motion against the blade, nipped the twine at the most economical point.

Jimmie worked his way down through the list, preparing each item as he read it, then methodically packed all parcels into two large corrugated cartons, asking Mick and me to carry them out one by one to the pony's cart. With our shopping list complete for this occasion, the manager, Mr. Wrafter, came to the outside of the counter, shook hands with all three, wished us the compliments of the season and handed Mother a nicely wrapped fruit cake as her Christmas box. In those marvellous days the Christmas box was standard practice even with the smaller shops. The bigger establishments usually presented a bottle of Port, a bottle of Sherry or a fruit cake, while the smaller concerns would never fail to hand out a packet of cigarettes, an ounce of tobacco, a mini box of chocolate or even a bar of scented soap.

With the cartons carefully stowed away under the straw, the pony securely tied and munching the last traneens of hay, we trotted off behind Mother to the Tullamore Drapery where she "had to get a few pairs of stockings and things." The thought uppermost in our minds was the inevitable visit to one of the many brightly lit toy shops. I knew she would eventually have to get Christmas stockings or other Santy items for the three youngest, Mick, Margaret and Tim. However, with the drapery purchases in her shopping bag it became clearly evident that the next port of call was Dann's tea shop in Bridge street.

"I don't know about you pair", she said, " but I'm parched for a cup o' tay, and that's what I'm goin' to get now."
On the way there we met Bridgie Kerwin, Fantin's daughter, who wished us all a happy Christmas, in her strong lilting voice, and insisted on "traitin' " us in Egan's snug, just across

the road from Dann's. Mother's protests went unheard, refusal was unacceptable.

"Ah! sure it's Christmas times", said Bridgie, "an' I'll bet the two lads haven't wetted their lips yet with a drop o' lemonade."

How right she was, we both gulped it down and had empty tumblers, long before they had consumed half their tiny glasses of Port.

"You're an awful girl, Bridgie," said Mother, "ye shouldn't have bothered wastin' yer money on us three, but now that we're here let me again wish happy Christmas to you and your father."

As the talk continued, discussions on recent funerals, future weddings, poor prices for farm produce and bad weather, our hunger pains grew keener. At long last when Bridgie refused to have a second Port, they both stood up, shook hands again wishing each other the compliments of the season for the third time. Bridgie then shook hands with Mick and me and at the same time, thrust a threepenny bit into our fists, winked and parted with the good humoured remark, "don't spend it all in the one shop, and keep an eye on yer mother, I think she's had one too many."

As we crossed the street, the extra money in our pockets felt reassuring. On every town trip we looked forward so much to visiting Dann's. They had lovely small cakes full of currants with lashings of pink icing on top, slabs of Chester cake, squares of apple tart, hot cross buns, plain buns with sticky crusts that looked like miniature batch loaves and even small packets of coconut biscuits for a penny.

We hastily made our way up the stairs, succeeding in our efforts to get a table near one of the front windows where we could look down on the street traffic below. Bernadette took our order and without much delay, arrived back carrying a tray on which she had set a large earthenware pot of tea, heavily muffled in a brown woollen tea cosy, a slice of appletart for Mother and two mouth-watering squares of Chester cake for us. Mick and I were ravenous, quickly clearing every crumb and then suggesting to each other in decibels loud enough for Mother to hear, that we should each spend our recent financial windfall on three packets of coconut biscuits. Realising the proposition was geared for her approval, she immediately responded, "Oh! ye can do what ye like with it, it's your money."

As it transpired, our eyes were bigger than our appetites, Mick only got through two packets while I failed to finish the third one. Mother paid the bill and much to our delight did not accept our biscuit contributions.

"I've to get a few Santy items for the three young ones, and a gansey for Christy" she said to me, out of earshot of Mick, as she made her way down the stairs, "I'm sure ye have something in mind yerselves before we head for home."

How right she was, Mick had set his heart on a little black gun. It was spring loaded and fired a slim pencil-like, wooden projectile which had a rubber suction cap at one end. When the suction cap was moistened with a lick of the tongue and fired at a door or smooth wall, it stuck firm and Mick was looking forward to some target practice on the barn door. He even threatened he might have a go at the grey gander, the one that always chased us flapping and hissing with neck outstretched, every time we ventured near the geese. All I wanted was a green steamroller which I had seen last year in McDonald's window, but did not have the necessary funds to make the purchase. This year the price had gone up by sixpence to three and sixpence. With the money I earned during the harvest at Kerwin's and Colton's jingling in my trouser pocket, I actually had one shilling and sixpence to spare. If the worst came to the worst I could extend a helping hand to Mick who only had a shilling and knew his gun was priced at two shillings. However, Mother had promised before we left for town, "she would help out Mick," and indeed came up trumps, despite her suggestion that "he might wait and see what Santy had up his sleeve before spending his own couple o' shillings." I had no delay at all in McDonald's, handing over my three shillings and sixpence and walking out carrying a shining new green steamroller, sporting two wide wheels at the back and a smooth grey roller in front, packed in its own box and neatly wrapped in brown paper. After waiting a full year to realise my dream I now felt like a millionaire and quite certain my elation at that moment, could not be exceeded today were somebody to present me with a new motor car.

Each clutching a parcel under our arm and wearing broad grins on our faces, we rejoined Mother in McFadden's drapery where she had collected her last remaining messages and appeared ready to set out for home.

"Begor, lookin' at the sparkles in yer eyes, it seems you pair got what ye wanted," she said, asking us at the same time to help her with some parcels across the street, to the pony's cart in Rhattigan's yard

"We did indeed, Mammy, we'll show them to you when we get home," enthused Mick, "we don't want to open the boxes now."

We then took her parcels and loaded them in under the straw, with the previous items. Kerry looked quite happy, still nibbling a mouthful of nice white hay which obviously had been given to him by some other farmer who tethered his pony nearby.

"Although it's freezin' cold, thank God the rain and sleet stayed away," said Mother as we drove out of Rhattigan's yard, turned right at Hayes' hotel and headed up High street on the road for home.

Mick and I had snuggled up as best we could in the straw at the back of the cart. We were very much aware we still had to pass Maggie Molloy's sweet shop out along the Clonminch road and I had a shilling left to spend. As we got within one hundred yards of the shop I tried a ploy which worked on previous occasions.

"If ye forgot any messages, loaves, candles or salt or anything, Mammy, ye'll be able to get them at Mag Molloy's."

"Well, God bless ye Tommy," she answered immediately, "for remindin' me. I want another red Christmas candle. They only had two left in O'Shaughnessy's and I intended getting a third. Slip in there and see if Mag has one," she said putting a two shilling piece in my hand, "and get a liquorice pipe or something for yerselves."

Mick winked at me and whispered, "Get something with yer own shilling as well."

While Mother pulled Kerry in tight to the kerb I jumped down and scampered into the shop. Maggie was a plump, grey haired, pleasant lady with bright blue eyes an infectious smile and not much taller than the counter.

"You're a son of Mary Ellen Murray, if she ever had one," said Maggie as I gave her my order for one Christmas candle, a square of Mickey Mouse toffee and two packets of ginger nuts.

"That's right," I answered, "my name's Tommy."

"Well you're the spittin' image o' yer mammy," said Maggie, "sure I knew all yer uncles out there in Cloncon and Killeenmore, I knew all the Caseys. Yer mother's name was Casey before she got married." she continued, as she took the square of Mickey Mouse toffee from a grey cardboard box and slipped it into a white paper bag with the two packets of ginger nuts. She then handed me the red Christmas candle rolled up in a sheet of brown wrapping. While I collected my change she persisted with a mini history of the Casey clan. Eventually I got a few words in edgeways and splurted out, "Well thanks very much Miss Molloy and a very happy Christmas."

As I skipped across to where Kerry was waiting with his patient passengers I could hear Maggie muttering some reference to "these youngsters nowadays, always in a hurry and runnin' and racin' ."

"She didn't keep ye too long," said Mother, "she's very friendly and an ould friend o' mine, I didn't think ye'd get out so quickly."

I hopped back up on the cart and proceeded to sort out my purchases. The square of Mickey Mouse toffee was sub-divided into twelve smaller squares, so I broke off a section of six and gave it to Mick together with a packet of ginger nuts. I gave Mother her change and we both gave her a ginger nut. Without looking over her shoulder to see what we were munching, she commented, "I'm glad ye got biscuits for yerselves and not some o' them ould hard toffees to damage yer teeth."

We looked at each other and remained culpably silent. As she tucked her navy blue scarf higher around her neck and urged Kerry into a steady trot, we burrowed our legs deeper into the straw to keep as warm as possible on the homeward trip.

Christmas Eve at last. Some few weeks ago it seemed like light years away, now the day had arrived and all the pent-up feelings of goodwill, hope and expectancy shone like beacons in every eye. A good mood prevailed as we diligently set about completing the Christmas chores for which the groundwork in many cases had already been laid. Yule logs, seasoning outdoors for the past two weeks were brought in to a special corner of the large kitchen. Sacks were filled with selected black turf and left ready for collection at a convenient point near the turf clamp. Stocks of turnips and mangolds in the pulper-house, for animal feed, were again checked and topped up if necessary as was the supply of potatoes in the barn for our own needs. We paid a visit to the bog and gathered sufficient long stemmed heather to make at least two new besoms and of course the fodderin' had to be attended to in the evening. In the meantime Mary decorated the kitchen, putting sprigs of red berried holly and sprays of ivy across the mantelpiece, over the doors and windows, behind the clock and every picture on the walls, not forgetting the Sacred Heart statue on the little shelf over mother's bed.

We all stuck willingly to our tasks in a very good-humoured way and helped each other out if one appeared to be falling behind. After tea the large galvanised bath tub went into overdrive as one by one we scrubbed and rinsed off all traces of the day's labour. Mother had to oversee the operation with the younger ones and ensure that knees, feet, neck and certain patches behind the ears were given the same attention as all other areas. Normally on Saturday nights each member of the family, old enough to do so, cleaned and polished his or her boots for Sunday Mass. But on this occasion Mary and I offered to polish and shine all footwear, so the freshly washed cherubs had no further opportunity of soiling themselves. Instead they got involved sorting out their clean stockings and hanging them at various vantage points for Santy. Bed time arrived earlier than usual for the three youngest, Mick, Margaret and Tim.

"There'll be no Santy Claus for you three, unless ye get to bed right away," said Mother. "Ye know he's outside listenin' to see who is up late."

As for the rest of us we had another hour or so before the rosary.

Christmas morning stole into the valley lit by a thousand stars. White hoary frost covered the ground and clung like strings of icing sugar to the twiggy shoots of the hawthorn and birch, giving the impression that a light coating of snow had fallen. Mick, Margaret and Tim had crept out of bed long before any of us wakened and their uncontrolled gasps of sheer delight, gave the message loud and clear that Santy had indeed paid a visit to the Murray household this year. A spinning top, two balloons and a Christmas stocking for Tim, aged five and a half. A brown school satchel with two exercise books in it, a writing case and a rag doll for Margaret, aged seven. Two pairs of grey woollen stockings with red diamonds on the fold and a hurley stick for Mick, aged eight and a half. The older three, Mary, Christy and I basked in the dubious glory of being "too big and ould to expect anything from Santy." Christy had already got his new shirt and red gallowses after the threshing, Mary a new school blouse and I got a pair of brown woollen gloves and two handkerchiefs. Shortly before seven o' clock Mother called Christy, Mick and me with the message to "hop out and get ready for eight o' clock Mass." Mary had already been given her brief to remain at home during first Mass, look after Tim and prepare the breakfast. She and Margaret would get a lift with Grandad to eleven o' clock Mass later.

At the outside it was no more than a twenty minute walk to St. Patrick's church in Killeigh village but Mother always insisted on giving herself half an hour, so needless to say we were ready by seven thirty, with peaked caps, hob nail boots and "shining morning faces." As we set out the air felt sharp and clear with a beautiful starry sky overhead. The hoary frost had caused some slippery patches on the road surface but not serious enough to hamper our brisk walk. Behind us in the distance, the clip clop of metal hooves echoed clearly through the crisp bracing air. Before long Dooley's pony and trap drew nearer, the faint yellow candle-light from the two coach lanterns contrasted sharply with the white glint of starlight. As they passed by Pat Dooley greeted us with, "Happy Christmas to ye all," and we replied in chorus, "Many happy returns."

That self same greeting and response, at times accompanied by a firm handshake, depending on the person and the circumstances, would be repeated over and over again while entering and leaving the church. Nearer to the village, Cruise's pony and trap and McDonald's side-car passed by, together with several neighbours on bicycles. Everyone felt joyful. Greetings were constantly exchanged and the feeling of goodwill was almost tangible. Eight o' clock Mass, always popular on Christmas morning, but we all hoped it wouldn't be Father Kennedy. His sermons were too wearisome and he tended to ramble and repeat himself. Like most country churches, there was no heating system of any kind and the temperature inside was just as cool, if not cooler than the air outside. Still, nobody gave the impression they were aware of the chill, it might even have been the opposite. A warm glow of benevolence and friendship permeated the hushed whispers of middle-aged fathers in navy blue suits, young mothers shepherding their brood and stout-hearted grandfathers with blackthorn sticks, as they shuffled towards the stone font, dipped their gnarled fingers in the holy water, made their way up the long aisle and then paused for a moment to bend the right knee as low as the arthritis would permit before entering their seat. Our fears of a long rambling sermon were allayed when we saw Father Prendergast emerge through the vestry door and after making the sign of the cross, intoned the opening words of the Introit, "Introibo ad altare Dei." His four young Mass servers responded, "Ad Deum qui laetificat juventutem meum."

The make-shift choir which had only come together for rehearsals in mid November, under the guidance of schoolteacher and organist, Mrs. Dowling gave quality performances of "Silent night" and "Adeste fideles." Father Prendergast, a tall friendly man with heavy eyebrows, a perpetual smile and a round fresh face much more akin to an overgrown schoolboy, than a middle-aged clergyman, treated us to a short meaningful homily on the true message of the nativity. With Mass over and before leaving the church, the handshakes and good wishes resumed, even with more vigour than when entering. These spontaneous, carefree, convivial gestures continued unabated as the folks from outlying districts like Killurin, Newtown and Derrybeg dawdled back to their ponies and traps and ponies and carts, safely hitched in Plunkett's or Mitchel's yard for the duration of Mass.

Back home, youngest brother Tim was still arranging

and re-arranging the contents of his Christmas stocking in a pile on the kitchen floor. A cardboard bugle, two aluminium cake dishes with a diameter no greater than a penny, a wooden hammer, a tiny mouth-organ with only three notes, a clown's paper hat and a small packet of coloured discs to be used in the snakes and ladders game, as outlined on one of the multicoloured stocking fillers. Margaret, proudly sporting her new brown school satchel had dressed her rag doll and was parading it up and down with the warning, "I have to get this baby asleep before I go to Mass." Much to Mother's delight, Mary had prepared the traditional tasty Christmas breakfast of pan-fried beef, black pudding and sausage together with tea and brown bread. A singular treat indeed for the Murray clan and a far cry from the everyday morning meal of bread, butter and tea. We had scarcely finished breakfast when the deep, warm melodious peals of the Church of Ireland bell rang out through the clear morning air, as it did every Sunday morning from the sylvan setting of Killeigh Abbey. In the Murray household we referred to it as the "half hour bell" because it sent out its clarion call to our Protestant neighbours half an hour before their service began, which by coincidence was also half an hour before the last Mass in St. Patrick's church. Even as it chimed our good friends Sam, Herbert and Tommy Matthews passed by in their pony and trap closely followed by Mrs. Colton with her sons John and Bertie.

"Are you two not ready for Mass yit, an' the "half hour bell" ringin' in the church lane for the last ten minutes?" enquired Mother, addressing Mary and Margaret.

"Ah mammy! it's only after startin' to ring a minute ago," protested Mary.

"Why can't ye be like those dedicated people gone

by in their ponies and traps," Mother continued, "and give yerselves plenty o' time instead of always rushin' out to your church at the last minute?"

Christy and I could scarcely hide the smiles. We ourselves had been on the receiving end of this very same challenge on many previous Sundays. However, this time it did goad the two girls into putting on a spurt and very soon they hopped up into the pony's cart and joined grandad on the short trip to eleven o'clock Mass. Mother then took advantage of one of her rare respites to sit down and read the current issue of the "Offaly Independent". I, as any big brother might do, busied myself demonstrating to little brother Tim, the intricacies of the spinning top. Mick and Christy collected a sliothar and went out to get the feel of Mick's new hurley in the first field.

The winter sun, although low in the south eastern sky had thawed irregular patches in the glistening white carpet of frost that covered the grass. Frost or no frost this did not deter the two hurlers as they each alternated the task of goalie with the role of full forward. When I eventually disentangled myself from the top-spinning lessons I joined the two sportsmen who promptly nominated me as goalie, while they launched a bombardment of close-in shots and long-distance high lobbing balls.

By the time our practice session finished, Mary had returned from Mass, slipped into her calico apron and started chopping onions, garlic, parsley and mint which, mixed with bread-crumbs and a few other ingredients, made up the stuffing. Mother, the only person who knew the recipe, handed down from her mother and grandmother before continued her work making and kneading that special dough paste, laced with spices and local herbs which she placed neatly over the sixteen pound goose in the medium sized skillet pot. This "goose paste" as we called it, which turned crispy brown when cooked, as well as tasting delicious also retained all the goodness and flavour of the meat, while absorbing the tang and piquancy of the complete dish. We were all warned earlier not to disappear or get lost out the fields as dinner would be ready around four o'clock. By half past three the hunger pains were so acute we had lost all interest in hurleys, spinning tops, rag dolls or steamrollers. Christy took a short cut to the haggard, lay down on a low bench of the hay rick and made a snug nest for himself, covering up legs, body and shoulders with loose dry hay. He looked so comfortable that Mick and I followed suit, making further dens for ourselves. Suddenly we heard some agitated squawking sounds emanating from the area of Mick's hideaway, "tcuk, tcuk," - tcuk, taw tcuk," "tcuk, tcuk, - tcuk taw tcuk." Then in a cloud of spores, hayseeds, dust and feathers, a White Wyandotte hen came fluttering out with wings flapping and high pitched cackling. She had obviously been "laying out" without anyone's knowledge and Mick's rummaging upset her nest which on closer inspection, yielded up its contents of seven eggs. This represented the second find of a hen "laying out" which we had stumbled on over the past three days. Christy had earlier found a Rhode Island Red shacked up with five eggs in the oaten straw rick. However, the current schamozzle had left us human nesters in some disarray, so we tidied the hay bench, collected the seven eggs and brought them in. Just in time too as Margaret was about to be despatched to "find them three buckos and tell them their dinner is gettin' cold."

Like the beef at breakfast, what a treat this pot-roast goose was to a family not all that familiar with meat at dinner time. As well as ducks and hens, Mother invariably kept a goose and gander, managing to rear five or six goslings each year, always keeping one for our own big day and from necessity, selling the remainder before Christmas. She killed and plucked the goose herself, then singed off the remaining pin-feathers over a blazing turf fire, cleaned out the "innards" and hung the bird from a rafter behind the kitchen door. Apart from the roast goose the Christmas dinner was a simple enough affair with home grown turnip, carrot or parsnip as vegetable and a plentiful supply of wholesome floury potatoes. Alcohol did not play a big part in our household. Grandad might have a bottle of porter before eating, or Mother a sip of the Port wine presented to her last year by Rhattigan's grocery, as a Christmas box. Likewise, there was no such course as dessert, sweet or afters. We did however finish with a cup of tea and a slice of Christmas cake.

With tummies full, Mary helped Mother tidy away the dinner plates in preparation for a big wash-up while the three big fellas coaxed the younger set to share their toys for a while. It wasn't the case that the boys wouldn't help with the wash-up but rather they were not allowed. Similar to the reasoning of so many other Irish mothers, washing up wasn't our job and anyway, we "would be trick actin' and smash some of the best plates and cups." Later in the evening when darkness had long since fallen and the kitchen lamp lit with its shining new globe, we were all thrilled to hear the metallic screech of the front gate being opened and see the flickering glow of a carbide lamp.

"Somebody should oil the hinges o' that gate," said Mother, "it makes my teeth water every time it's opened."

It was indeed our uncle Mike, he loved coming to our

house at Christmas, "to have a bit of fun with the kids" and I suppose, in his heart of hearts, to play with the toys. He showed us many tricks with cards and last year we had a long enjoyable session of "twenty fives." Mike was a bachelor who delighted to be with children in the Santa Claus season, especially when the children were his own nieces and nephews. He had a marvellous way with young people, loved telling yarns, teasing and carrying on with pseudo cheating at card games in which we all delighted. He had a highly infectious hearty laugh, often leaving him and us with tears streaming down our faces and even Mother in the background was not immune. This year was no different, as he entered the door and left his carbide lamp on the kitchen dresser, he handed a brown paper parcel to Mary whom he dubbed "Mariah", saying with a glint in his eye, "That's your Christmas box Mariah." As this had never happened before, Mary naturally expressed surprise, muttered a shy, "Thanks very much Mike" and opened the small odd-shaped packet to find a pencil pushed through the core of an empty wooden thread spool. With the forced effort of a girl who knew she'd been duped, Mary grinned, "Well thanks for nothing," as uncle Mike positively doubled up laughing and the rest of us quickly followed suit.

"I'll tell you one thing," said Mary, looking at her erstwhile benefactor, "you'll get a nice Christmas box from me next year."

When he recovered his equilibrium, Mike pulled up a chair to the open fire and held out his hands to the warm flames.

"Bloody cowld ould night out there," he said, alternatively rubbing his hands together and then holding them close to the flames again.

"Bloody cowld," he repeated, "but hardy and dry. Where's the ould fella?" he enquired, referring to grandad.

"Oh! he rambled down as far as Purcell's," replied Mother, "sure ye might have guessed," she continued, "this gang wouldn't be carryin' on like that if he was here."

And how right she was, we had long since accepted that unlike uncle Mike he wasn't particularly fond of young people and he worked totally on the basis that they should be seen but never heard. His first commandment for children appeared to be, "All work and no play is the right medicine everyday." We would indeed have been delighted had he "rambled down" to Purcell's every night, and I'm sure Mother would not have been too perturbed either.

"I suppose ye wouldn't say no to a bottle o' stout?" suggested Mother, as she approached uncle Mike with a bottle in one hand, a corkscrew and a blue and white mug in the other.

"Begob yer a dowser," said Mike, as he accepted, "sure maybe it might hate me up."

Without delay he pulled the cork, poured out the dark brown liquid and holding the mug aloft wished us all a merry Christmas. After taking one or two mouthfuls he poured the remainder of the bottle into the mug, wiped the creamy froth from his lips and with a twinkle in his eye told us he had a good story about a young lad who answered an advertisement which called for "a responsible boy." Mike continued, "and what gives you the idea you're responsible?" asked the prospective employer. "Well," said the young lad, "in any of my previous jobs, when anything went wrong the boss always told me I was responsible."

Mike laughed so heartily at his own joke that his merriment became so contagious we all broke down. When he regained his composure he suggested, "What about an ould game o' cards?" This was greeted with a chorus of yesses, so he continued, "Of course nobody can play unless they've money because it's a penny all in."

Any of us with sixpences or threepenny bits rushed to change the coins into pennies and others with cash flow problems had to negotiate quick loans.

Probably the most popular card game in the midlands, and the game uncle Mike loved best was "twenty fives." Before starting he gave us a quick run-down on the card values. The joker headed the list, followed by the five of trumps, knave of trumps, ace of hearts, ace of trumps and king and queen of trumps. For the numbered cards, the value sequence lay in the highest in red and the lowest in black. Mary found all this far too taxing on the memory, quickly scribbled down most of the data in her best shorthand and pleaded with us not to complain if she made a mistake. It soon became apparent her uptake had developed sharper than ours. As the games progressed, it transpired she made less blunders than we did. Nevertheless the enjoyment kept bubbling especially when one of us, with the last throw of the game, succeeded in playing a Knave of trumps or an ace of hearts to prevent Mike, already sitting on twenty, from getting the final trick with his King of trumps. He obviously enjoyed all this as much as we did. When the tables were turned and he had the winning card for the final trick, he'd stand up with tears of mirth streaming down his face and smack his King, Queen or ace off the table before bending over in laughter. Then the hilarity and merriment repeated when Mike caught one of us either intentionally, or unintentionally reneging. It was wonderful to witness the pleasure he took in seeing his nine of diamonds win a trick against our King or Queen because we had reneged on his Knave in an earlier lead.

The glee and gaiety continued unabated for almost two and a half hours. By that time all the young folk had run short of pennies on three or four occasions and made hasty trips to a reasonably disposed Banker, now busy in the kitchen preparing tea and a slice of Christmas cake for the gamblers. Uncle Mike who won most of the games totted up his hoard. He stacked the pennies in piles of twelve, then teasingly counted out the windfall.

"One shilling, two shillings, three shillings, four shillings; four shillings and ninepence, not a bad bit o' profit at all," said Mike, with a wry smile.

"I hope yer not cheatin' or robbin' those youngsters," said Mother, winking at Mary.

Of course Mike wasn't really serious and took pleasure watching our reactions. When the cards were cleared away and all had partaken of tea and Christmas cake, Mike rearranged his money piles and handed each of his four erstwhile henchmen one shilling and twopence, keeping a penny for himself to even things out. Everybody ended up happy and the young folk now had more money than when they started.

"I'd hate to break up yer fun on a Christmas night, but don't ye think it's gettin' near bed time?" suggested Mother, "ye were all up early for Mass this morning."

"Begob, it's time for me to make a move too", said Mike, "I didn't realise it was so near to twelve, I suppose all good things must come to an end."

Never one to dilly-dally at a late hour, he stood up smiled at us all, donned overcoat, scarf and cap, collected his bicycle lamp from the dresser and told us to keep all our money for the next game.

"Sure yer time enough, Mike," said Mother, "it's ony these young ones I'm bothered about, an' I'll make ye a quick cup o' tea before ye leave."

But Mike was having none of it. "No, not at all", he said, "sure it's not long since I had a cup, anyway it's too near midnight for tea, I'll hit the road."

Conditions outside were cold and the light from a million twinkling stars, made scant intrusion on the all-enveloping darkness.

"Go off in out of the cowld, it's goin' to freeze cats and dogs later on," advised Mike as he bade farewell to us all and tucked in the tails of his overcoat on the bicycle saddle before fading into the obscure landscape and merging with the darkness.

Eleven o' clock chimed on St. Stephen's day before the first gang of Wren Boys arrived. There were four of them in the group, four males dressed up in their mother's or sister's most colourful apparel of yesteryear. Wearing various items of headgear, peaked caps, woollen berets and felt hats, all had their faces painted or wore vizards. The leader carried a tin can for donations and a holly bush alive with red berries and decorated with multi-coloured ribbons. Christy and I had had our breakfast but some of the sleepy heads just tumbled out of bed when they heard the Wren Boys chant:-

Wren the wren the king of all birds,
St. Stephen's Day she was caught in the furze.
Although she was caught her family was great,
So rise up good lady and give us a trate.
All silver and no brass,
Help the Wren to get a glass.
We hunted her up and we hunted her down,
We hunted her into Killeigh town.

At that point Mother rattled three pence into the cocoa tin they carried as a collection box. Each one of the four thanked her, wished us a very prosperous New Year and headed off on bicycles to their next engagement. Throughout the day we had visitations from a further six groups, although some were not as professional as our first visitors. In fact the second gang were neighbours' children, no more than ten or eleven years old and travelling on shank's mare. Nevertheless, they got their two pence or three pence and went happily on their way. The Wren Boys dress and modus operandi resembled that of the Pookas at Halloween, except the Pookas carried musical instruments, melodeons, mouth organs, bodhrans or tamboreens and played music. The Wren boys on the other hand sported a holly bush with an ample supply of red berries, decorated with multicoloured streamers and possibly including something to represent an effigy of a dead wren while they rendered their special rhyme. We never left the house all day long, waiting with childish curiosity to see if we knew who the next visitors were and to gape in wonderment at their trappings and garb.

As we reached the final days of December, Christmas and St. Stephen were, of course, now further away than ever. Winter tightened its grip and the first wisps of snow were visible on the north ridge of Arderin, the highest peak in the Slieve Bloom mountains.

"Aw! don't mind those few patches on the high ground," said Mother, "it's not goin' to snow, it's far too cowld, it's goin' to stay frosty."

That sounded like good news to us because the drinking pond in the corner of Clooney's field had been frozen over with thick ice for the past three days. Clooney's field and the adjoining Well field were pastures and each evening we had the opportunity of a few slides on the frozen pond, before driving home the cows for milking. To supplement this we also spilled a few bucketfuls of water on the road outside our home and made a slide almost thirty yards long. This worked out very well, being near the house we were allowed to stay out later at night, especially if we were blessed with the light of the moon. Christy, Mick and I were able to go the full length on our hunkers. On the odd occasion, after generating some extra speed, one of us might tumble over backwards and skid to a halt on our backsides. Being on our hunkers we hadn't far to fall, never got hurt and the tumble only added to the fun. Despite the wear and tear on clothing and footwear, Mother never really complained. We were at home and in earshot of the house. If she objected to us sliding there, she knew we might put up strong arguments to be allowed cycle to Pallas lake near Tullamore, or maybe sneak off to Pallas when her back was turned. This would really worry her because in previous years Pallas had proved dangerous with near fatal incidents when the ice broke.

With the continued covering of heavy frost on the ground, the food supply for robins, blackbirds, sparrows and finches diminished daily. Periodically we threw out a spoonful of porridge, breadcrumbs or even potato skins from the dinner table, but they were invariably gobbled up by the larger birds, crows, jackdaws and starlings. Of course marauding gangs of our own hens, ducks and geese didn't help the situation either. Mike Casey had shown us how to catch small birds with a crib made totally from fine hazel wattles. The finished object looked like a miniature pyramid with an open square base, then tapering to a height of approximately eight to ten inches. When set, it was propped up on one side with an ingenious release device, which rested against a trip roost just inside the crib. As mentioned it was made entirely from hazel shoots and we used breadcrumbs or oatmeal as a lure. Once the robin or blackbird entered, it couldn't get the food morsels without depressing the trip roost, then the prop collapsed and the crib dropped, catching our little feathered friend inside. We usually left the captive there for a short while, hoping he'd settle and eat some of the breadcrumbs, then release him and re-set the crib to catch and feed another. We obviously didn't have enough sense to realise the little creatures were far too scared to eat anything in captivity.

5 Sliding to school

There was nothing special about New Year's day, just another Holy day of obligation and we all had to go to Mass as we did on a normal Sunday. There were no traditional celebrations in the area on New Year's eve and of course television, as we know it now, had not yet been invented. Only the odd family with money to spare for luxuries could afford to own and service a wireless. I had no idea of the intricacies of the wireless then and am still no wiser today, but I knew it needed two batteries, a dry battery and a wet battery. Doubtless, conditions were different for families who lived in towns and cities where electricity formed part and parcel of everyday life. Rural electrification still ambled along in it's infancy, so paraffin lamps and wireless sets with wet and dry batteries, remained very much alive and well in country districts.

Monday the second day of January the frosty conditions eased somewhat, the wind had moved round to the north east and predictions began to look more and more like snow. The small white patches on the Slieve Blooms had now knitted together to form an almost unbroken blanket and not surprisingly, before nightfall all roads and fields were covered to a depth of three inches. By Tuesday the wind had veered to a more easterly direction, and according to Mother, that would bring black frost during the day with no hope of a thaw. How right she was, more snow fell during the night and it now lay firm and deep under foot. As we were still on school holidays, Christy, Mick and I got our hands on an old part-rusty sheet of corrugated iron, which had been replaced on the roof of the pony shed. This was to be our snow sleigh.

By stomping on it with our feet we broadly succeeded in bending one end upwards. The bent portion would act as a foot rest and prevent the lead end of the corrugated sheet from digging into the snow.

There were no hills or slopes of any significance on our own farm so carrying the "sleigh" over our heads like a currach, we crossed the road and made our way to Fletcher's second field. The hill here had a reasonably good gradient. With two bodies on board at a time the extra weight succeeded in generating an acceptable speed for the short downhill run. We never tired hauling the corrugated sheet back up the slope to repeat the descent, time and time again. Eventually darkness closed in on us and that session, reluctantly, had to be abandoned.

By the end of the week there was still no sign of a thaw and Saturday's "Offaly Independent" informed us that Tullamore and surrounding districts, were suffering from an almost unprecedented spell of frost and snow. Some roads were snowbound and practically impassable. Frozen water mains were badly affecting supplies to homes and business premises in the town. By contrast, the news for the younger folk on Monday turned out to be good. Killurin school was not opening and would remain closed until further notice. Mother wasn't too happy about this. Already overtaxed, drying out trousers and ganseys from slides and snow-fights she now saw no respite on the horizon. However, the situation did improve, within a few days a thaw set in, the snow disappeared and Killurin school re-opened but just as quickly the frosty conditions returned. Nevertheless, so long as she could "get you gang out from under me feet and back to school," she was happy. Unfortunately, it transpired other essential humanitarian exercises needed attention. On our first day back to school, Mr. Hutton informed us that it was the turn of the Murray family to supply a load of turf for school heating. The practice of course was that all families who owned turf banks had to provide fuel for school heating from October to March and it was now our stint.

With the fun we were having on our make-shift ice rinks, the January days drifted by quickly. Christmas holidays were well and truly over but with icy roads still available all the way to Killurin school, the normally tiresome journey now took on a whole new meaning and seemed much more interesting especially on the homeward run. There were smashin' long slides at McDonald's gate, down the hill at Brazil's, on the level stretch outside Kelly's and again all the way from Heffernan's to Kenna's cottage.

Sunday night and two weeks into January, we noticed Mother reading the Christmas number of "Irelands' Own". We suddenly realised, because of all the festive celebrations and seasonal diversions, a most important and enjoyable feature had somehow been overlooked. She had not read for us the latest adventures of "Kitty the Hare." The reading of this highly entertaining ghost story from each issue of "Irelands' Own", from the time we were all very young, was almost a religious practice in our home. Obviously, she herself, enjoyed the well written stories too as she gathered the six of us around the fireside and took pleasure in interpreting the cadences and rhythms in the unmistakeable terminology of author, Victor O. D. Power. "Kitty the Hare" used wonderful descriptive language which almost gave the story a third dimension:- ".....Begannies, with the dint of the cold shivers darting up and down his spine like needles he stood motionless in terror, while the November wind moaned like banshees through the tall elm trees, that lined the long dark winding avenue, leading to the big house". ...

Vivid, expressive descriptions like this were masterly interwoven in every episode and we often thought the longer the sentence the more pleasure Mother got from reading it.

To get the story in motion on this occasion, it didn't take too much encouragement on our part.

"Oh, indeed I'll read it for ye alright," agreed Mother, "as soon as I browse through the other items."

And true to her word, without any undue delay she did treat us to another heartwarming and gripping instalment in the life of "Kitty the Hare". Amazingly, the stories never really scared us although at times we did innocently deliberate whether some of the happenings, as recounted, could actually occur to us in our own day to day life before finally falling asleep. I suppose the fact that the three of us eldest lads bunked in together in the press-bed, gave us more courage than if we slept in a room on our own. Being in the press-bed, which of course in the daytime folded back into a press-like wardrobe also helped. With its roof or canopy overhead and its two side wings, our imagination had less chance of picking out dark objects in the room to convert into ghosts or spooks.

The third week in January heralded the end of the snow. Heavy rain took its place and together with the melting slush caused floods in many places. The next ten days saw many surprising and abrupt changes in weather conditions which caused Grandad to growl:-

"Well, be the hevers o' war, I often heard the ould sayin', 'March many weathers', but ye could certainly slap it on January, this year."

The rain was followed by frost then back to wind and

rain again, to be replaced a second time by frost, eventually turning to further falls of snow which lasted until the end of the month. Because of the weather conditions, January came to a close with little or no activity on the farms. This did not at all mean farmers were enjoying a well earned rest. Before the snow arrived, Kellys had finished off a long delayed fencing job along their bog fields with oak stakes and barbed wire. Mike Casey working in his all purpose barn, made four complete new wooden gates for the outlying pastures at the Cloncon end of his farm and Purcells succeeded in putting in a new bridge on the access road to their turf bank, using old railway sleepers and many loads of river gravel.

6   Helping the Thatcher

What better way to introduce February than a few lines from Francis Ledwidge's poem, - "Evening in February."

> The windy evening drops a grey
> Old eyelid down across the sun,
> The last crow leaves the ploughman's way
> And happy lambs make no more fun.
> Wild parsley buds beside my feet,
> A doubtful thrush makes hurried tune,
> The steeple in the village street,
> Doth seem to pierce the twilight moon.

La Fheile Bhride, Saint Brighid's Day, the first of February and the first day of spring. Saint Brighid, Ireland's second patron saint who, according to legend, promised the weather would improve from her day onward. In certain parts of the country Saint Brighid's Day was celebrated as a Holy Day but not in our parish. Similarly we had no great tradition in the making of Saint Brighid's crosses throughout the Killeigh area. However, from the grown-up's point of view, this year, whether Saint Brighid had a hand in it or not, there certainly seemed to be an improvement in the weather. Snowdrops peeped out from their little nests underneath the currant bushes and a genuine feeling of spring pervaded the air. But to us the first of February caused some disappointment. It ushered in the end of the snow skiing and sliding. The day dawned bright and mild with a soft westerly breeze setting in a quick thaw, which in a few short hours gently bared erratic strips of green grass down through our erstwhile ski slopes in Fletcher's field. Likewise a film of water from melting ice, settling on the surface of our once strong skating rink, now proved to be a tell-tale sign that another area of winter sports was fading fast.

The newly arrived mild weather heralded a bout of 'flu which closed schools in the Kilcormac area but thankfully did not affect anybody in our household except Grandad. He stayed in bed for four or five days with little or no appetite, mother had to make his favourite tea-time tit-bit, buttermilk stirabout. This porridge made from full-grain oatmeal, cooked in fresh buttermilk rather than water, established itself as a firm favourite with some of us young folk, especially the lads. So much so that Mick in his innocence, passed the remark, "I hope Grandad stays sick for a good few weeks, so we can keep on getting buttermilk stirabout". However, to assist the recuperating process and help clear the lung congestion, mother decided to produce a mugful of buttermilk gruel on two or three occasions each day. The gruel by tradition had to be made in a large enamel "burner" and kept continually hot on a nest of turf coals on the hob. As a matter of interest, all saucepans, whether for cooking vegetables, chickens or rice, were known as burners - the small burner, the big burner, the enamel burner, etc. as the case demanded. During his sickness Grandad had asked us to keep an eye on the snares and the fox trap he had set in the ditch between the Turn field and the moor. All of us had at times heard the chilling yelp of foxes, as they stealthily lurked and roamed under the cover of winter darkness. As usual at this time of the year the frost and snow made it much more difficult for them to sustain their food supply line. In mid-January, two of the more daring had netted a pair of prize chickens, coming right up to the hen-house, during the night on one occasion and picking off the second in the haggard in broad daylight. Heartbreaking episodes for Mother and understandably she totally agreed with fox traps being set to catch the culprits. Snaring rabbits, to supplement the fresh meat supply, the only meat source for several families, was practiced extensively. As well as catering for home needs, a steady market existed in Tullamore for rabbit meat. Indeed some families depended more on this activity for income than on the meagre earnings from their farms.

The first day we checked the traps and snares for Grandad we had nothing to report but our second day's surveillance heralded some good news for Mother. Although the traps were all empty a fox had somehow got himself caught in one of the rabbit snares. As we stared at this beautiful clever creature of the wild lying so still and motionless on the slopes of a grassy bank, a bank he must surely have considered part of his own private domain, our gut feeling seemed to be one of sorrow. Sorrow, because now, in hindsight, it all seemed so simple for us and so unfair to him. He had crept to an untimely death with little odds in his favour. However, when we arrived home carrying our victim, Mother had a different line of thought.

"Well, more power t'yer elbows, lads!," she enthused, "that'll keep that fella quiet! now he wont be so bloomin' quick gettin' his next chicken dinner".

Then addressing me directly, she advised,

"You can get a spade, Tommy, and bury him in the corner of Clooney's field, down near the bog gate."

By the time we collected the spade from the barn and thrown the corpse into a boxbarrow, the three of us were joined by schoolmates, Con and Charlie Kelly, who happened to be passing by. They heard "the commotion in Murray's yard" and wanted to join the ranks of this curious, ragtag funeral cortege as it set off on its journey to complete the final act in the lifespan of an unlucky member of the Reynard family.

The February weather continued to remain mild and dry. Joe Fletcher, always out of bed before cock-crow, got himself organised early for his trip to "Donegal". On arrival there he yoked his graceful team of two red mares, to the swing plough and "in God's name" turned the first brown sod of the year in that bumpy, undulating field he affectionately called "The red hill". The soil was indeed a reddish brown and with the uneven texture of the field, Joe decided to use his swing plough. The swing plough had no wheels and its easily adjustable draught, operated by the plough handles, made it most suitable for hilly and undulating surfaces. Joe had already "stepped" the field and marked out the headlands so he knew exactly where to open the first of two middles. He had only ploughed three or four scrapes when his plot fell prey to a bevy of noisy crows, intermingled with a scattering of gulls, all keeping a safe distance behind as they sought out and challenged for each newly-stripped morsel. Joe soon had built up ten or twelve perfectly straight scrapes on either side of the middle and on one occasion as he turned his team on to the headland, stopped and looked back to admire his work.

"Damn it!" said Joe to himself, "that's nice, well-turned straight ploughing."

Then with a smile developing beneath a neatly trimmed moustache, he continued, "Ye know I should be at the ploughing match in Birr today, I'd bate the best o' them."

Well, indeed, weather conditions at Eglish, Birr, were ideal for the County Ploughing Championships and Joe was to find out later that our cousin, John Casey of Cloncon, won first prize while his great rival Matt Meleady of Ballydaly, took second place. John also won best middle.

In the meantime back at our own home, Fantin Kerwin called to advise he intended starting "that thatching job" on our dwelling house on Saturday, a task he found impossible to fit in before Christmas. The thatching operation, by tradition, usually took place during winter months. It didn't make sense to encourage this undertaking in spring, summer or autumn when farmers should be ploughing, tilling, cutting turf, making hay or saving the harvest. The fact that he had nominated a date, represented good news and something we were expecting to hear for some time. Grandad, now well recovered from his bout of 'flu, had spent a full day cutting and pointing hazel scollops.

Fantin arrived good and early on this mild and calm Saturday morning knowing we had no school and "the young lads will be there to give me a bit o' help pullin' thatch and handin' up scollops." Unfortunately he brought with him the sad tidings that the Pope, Pope Pius XI, had died the previous day, the tenth of February. Mother had not heard the news and appeared very upset.

"Well there's one thing for sure, he's gone straight to heaven," she said as she regained her composure.

"Aye indeed", agreed Fantin, "he was a saintly man."

We liked Fantin, got on well with him and looked forward to his arrival. After all, wasn't it he and Cluck Dunne who usually gave us the egg cups full of porter at the thrashin'? For us the thatching job held its own fascination, it gave us an excuse to climb to the top of the roof on the ladder, on the pretext we were helping the thatcher. There was also the likelihood we would earn a slice of applecake with the eleven o' clock tay. The applecake - Mother's creation could never be described as an apple tart. Made in the same baker which she used for brown bread, it had a deep, soft juicy base and a thick wavy top crust. It totally deserved its title. Mother usually baked this apple cake or rhubarb cake when we had a craftsman like Fantin working on some special undertaking.

The previous day while we were at school Grandad had actually started the operation by shaking out some sizeable heaps of oaten straw, then damped the piles down using several bucketsful of water. With the straw reasonably wet he placed weights in the form of short planks or bricks on top to keep the pile rigid during the "pulling" exercise. As Christy and I moved in to play our part Fantin advised us,

"Whin you're pullin' thatch lads, take fairly small amounts at a time, pull from the bottom o' the stack, pull steadily to allow the straw to come out straight and unbroken, don't chuck. Then carefully swish aich handful agin that plank there, to knock off the excess water, place yer handful on that rope on the ground and repeat the exercise a few times. Whin ye have a nice shaveful, tie the rope and carry it up to me."

After a few mediocre starts we got the hang of it, got the rhythm right, and Fantin appeared quite pleased with the result. He took an armful of the newly pulled thatch together with a dozen scollops and mounted the ladder, going just slightly above the eave. He stuck three scollops into the old thatch about nine or ten inches apart and used them as a buttress to hold the armful of thatch and the remainder of the scollops in a working position. Then he immediately

Master Thatcher, Christy Brereton, doing the final trim after finishing a job at Geashill, Offaly, in 1983. (Courtesy: John Kearney, Offaly Historical and Archaeological Society Tullamore)

descended, collected his wooden mallet, his short thatching rake, a further bundle of scollops and mounted the ladder once more.

Christy and I were going well with the "pulling" job and realised as soon as Fantin got into his stride, the demand for new thatch would be unrelenting. Nevertheless we took a short break to witness the start-up. With all items at the ready and the ladder resting flat against the old roof, two or three feet from the gable end barge, Fantin placed his first handful of golden oaten straw in position, spreading it out over a width of about twelve to fourteen inches, leaving the loose ends dangling down well over the existing eave. He laid a scollop across the span of new thatch, inserting the two pointed ends deep into the old roof to keep the pile firm. He then took a second scollop, rested the centre against the side of the wooden ladder, gave it a solid thump with his mallet taking care not to break or sever it but to leave the damaged area pliable and fibrous. By holding one end and twisting the other, using the soft centre as a pivot, he folded over the scollop to form an elongated U and then hammered in this wooden staple to pin the first scollop tightly against the thatch and repeated the performance with a second wooden staple.

He proceeded by placing a second portion of thatch in position, this time making certain that the bottom half of the new section covered the top half of the first section as well as concealing the clamping scollops he had just hammered in. Fantin continued the sequence with each new section, until step by step upwards he reached the highest point on the roof, then came back down to the eave to commence a new course. Having witnessed the thatcher's craft at first hand for some time, Christy and I returned to replenishing and building up new stocks of thatch. On a few occasions during the day as Fantin completed a wide span of five or six feet, he sprinkled the area with water, raked it in downward strokes with his thatching rake to align and straighten all individual straws and this in turn promoted the downward flow of subsequent falls of rainwater. Thatchers in the midlands had a preference for oaten straw, being less brittle than wheat or barley stalks, it had a flatter or wider stem and of course the golden colour always proved to be most attractive. At the end of the day one quarter of the roof basked in a new thick coat of yellow flaxen thatch and after four days, the assignment, to coin a suitable phrase, was wrapped up.

Fantin actually finished early on the fourth day and before dusk fell, had time to trim the fringe of jagged straws protruding over the eaves with the aid of a sheep shears. The finished article looked extremely smart and provoked Grandfather into mumbling that this final tonsorial escapade, "made the ould house look as if it was sportin' a smartly trimmed moustache". The rear of our home had been thatched a year earlier so all sections of the roof were now watertight for at least another decade.

After tea Fantin promised he would drop in on us for an hour on the following Monday to water down the new thatch with a mixture of bluestone and washing soda. This was part of the thatcher's job, the application successfully curbed the growth of oat seeds or weeds which might have survived. Indeed he advised that if possible, the treatment should be applied annually, it would in later years revive the colour of the thatch as well as killing off weeds and other unwanted growth.

"Begob! they're two bully lads," he said to Mother, before leaving, "they'll make thatchers in no time."

Then putting his hand in his trouser pocket, he took out a coin and gave it to me.

"Did ye ever see anythin' like that before?" he enquired.

"Indeed I did, sure it's only a shillin,' but it's new an' shiny," I answered.

"Are ye sure?" said Fantin, "have a look at both sides."

I turned it over a few times, the bull looked as it always did, but the harp side appeared somewhat different, although I couldn't pinpoint what it was.

"That's one of our new coins," said Fantin, "they've only come out in the last few days. Bridgie got two in Tullamore; they've "Eire" on the harp side instead of "Saorstat Eireann."

After a further inspection and a short history discussion, I went to hand it back to Fantin, but he pushed it away saying, "Put it in yer pocket and keep it Tommy, and while ye have it, ye'll always have money."

"Begor, there's a great chance o' that happenin' ", said Mother dubiously, as she bid farewell to Fantin, "with Ash Wednesday comin' up on the twenty second, I'm sure they'll spend every penny they have before Lent."

Lent was a time of genuine fast for everyone over seven years of age. Only one full meal each day, no meat on Fridays and there appeared to be an almost compulsory onus on children to give up sweets and biscuits until Easter, with a possible break for Saint Patrick's day. So any spare money they might have had, "burned a hole in their pockets" as Mother said until they spent it before Ash Wednesday.

As we drifted through the remaining days of February the daily trudge to and from Killurin school became less dreary and was brightened somewhat by the growing numbers of baby lambs frisking and frolicking in several fields along the route. While the younger lambs kept close to their mother, the older ones were in no way shy and might be persuaded, with a little patience, to suck the fingers of some outstretched hand through the bars of the field gate. Always fascinating to young eyes, watching these lithe woolly pets as they hopped, skipped and bounced around before diving at their mother's milk supply, to puck and feed while tails wagged furiously in a display of sheer joie-de-vivre.

7 The crows start to build

With only days to go before the first of March, an intense upsurge in both the number of crows and the decibels of their noisy activity became quite evident as they cawed, wheeled and weaved a black blanket in the air, before settling in pairs high up in the tall pines and beeches. In the interests of accuracy, I think it would only be fair comment to point out at this juncture that the birds we all referred to as crows were in fact rooks.

Mother suggested, "with all this hustle and bustle there must be a storm coming up,"

Grandad countered, "Not at all child! don't ye know the crows always start building their nests on the first day o' March, and they traditionally carry on cawin' an' courtin' an' pairin' off like that, a few days beforehand." He continued, "Ye know when the first of March falls on a Sunday, the crows never build until the followin' day."

We were sorry we couldn't check out his theory, as we knew the first of March would fall on a Wednesday. Sure as goodness, as Wednesday dawned we honestly believed the cawing had reached a new crescendo and passing the tall trees near Brazil's old house on our way to school, we noticed several crows arriving with twigs in their beaks and landing in the top-most branches. As the days passed the flutter and flapping of wings continued, and soon bulky, gangly nests took shape in the tree-tops. The cawing and commotion persisted unabated for another eight to ten days. After further careful scrutiny of the new aerial homesteads, it was clearly evident the females were well into their laying and hatching season while the males were making their best efforts to be dependable guardians and supportive parents. We concluded that at least Grandad's theory regarding the crows starting to build on the first of March was correct and we gave him the benefit of the doubt as far as the Sunday work was concerned.

At school Mr. Hutton asked us if we knew that a new Pope had been elected, taking the name Pius XII. We had heard Grandad discussing the system of election and how white smoke from some chimney gave the signal that the Cardinals had reached a conclusion. However, only two or three in the class could remember what name he had taken. Mr. Hutton also told us the result of the election was known immediately far beyond the Vatican, because radio had been used for the first time to give the news.

> Within the oak a throb of pigeon wings
> Fell silent, and grey twilight hushed the fold,
> And spiders' hammocks swung on half-oped things
> That shook like foreigners upon the cold.
> A Gipsy lit a fire and made a sound
> Of moving tins, and from an oblong moon
> The river seemed to gush across the ground
> To the cracked metre of a marching tune.

(An extract from "A Twilight in Middle March", by Francis Ledwidge.)

With mid March approaching and an all round increase in bird-song, there's a great feeling of spring in the air. Ploughing and tilling for corn crops, wheat, barley and oats as well as root crops, potatoes, beet and turnips is now in full swing. Jim Connolly is tilling a dry field of lea which

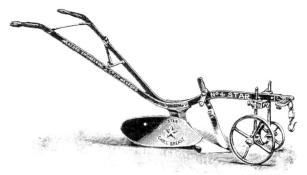

The popular "Pierce" plough as used widely in the Midlands in the 1930's.
(Courtesy: Wexford County Library)

he ploughed last week. This ground in the three previous years had produced successive crops of hay and was now being prepared for a spring sowing of feeding barley. As is sometimes the case with ploughed lea, the sod remained lumpy and knobbly. Even after harrowing it in both directions he still had to use his metal roller and then harrow it a third time. Like many other small farmers we only had a stone roller, pedestrian operated, while Jim's metal roller was accommodated with a sturdy seat to use while driving it.

In the adjoining field Freddie Colton grubbing stubbles with a spring-grub, seemed almost invisible in a

Stone Roller.
(Courtesy: Department of Irish Folklore, University College Dublin)

flutter of black and white wings, as crows and gulls circled and hovered, scanning the newly disturbed soil for any tasty tit-bits. On our way home from school we stopped to peep in at the proceedings and shouted a loud, "God bless the work."

"You too", came the answer, "an' maybe if you lads did a bit o' work for me, He'd bless that as well."

"We wouldn't be able to do that kind o' job for ye," chimed Christy, nodding his head towards the grub while at the same time knowing quite well that wasn't what Mr. Colton had in mind.

"Well, I had a lot o' trouble with scutch grass in this field, last year," said Freddie, as he steered his agile team on to the headland. "When I get it ploughed, I'll give it another run or two with the spring-grub, a deep harrowin' to bring the scutch to the top, then I'll run over it with the chain-harrow."

"I suppose that's where we come in," I suggested.

"Yer dead right Tommy, I'd be delighted if ye could give me an evenin' or two pickin' the scutch, puttin' it into little hapes an' burnin' it."

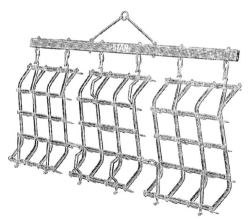

Zig-Zag steel harrow.
(Courtesy: Irish Agricultural museum, Johnstown Castle, Wexford)

He looked at us for a moment anticipating an answer, and then continued, "O' course ye'll get one and thruppence a day for yer efforts; what d' ye think lads?"

The one and thruppence a day was the news we were waiting to hear, and as we always found the smell of burning scutch most appealing we agreed and told Freddie we'd be ready and eager as soon as he had the field chain-harrowed.

Dawdling on homewards near our own house we passed Ber Butler and a gang of road workers, "road min", as everyone called them, complete with rusty metal barrows, spades, shovels and the inevitable pile of river gravel. They were trimming the grass verges with spades and filling in pot-holes with the gravel. We often wondered why the "road min" spent days and weeks on this job as the filling only remained in position for a very short while before being washed out with heavy rain, or dispersed in all directions under the wheels of Bill Feehan's chicken van, or the red oil lorry delivering paraffin and other oils to Buckley's shop. As we drew near, Ber Butler handed me a coal-black billy-can with the request:-

"Would ye get yer mother to fill that with boilin' water, Tommy; we'll be stoppin' in a minute or two to make a cup o' tay, an' I'll collect it from her then."

This scenario had occurred many times in the past and Mother knew exactly what to do. When she became aware there were "road min" in the vicinity she arranged to keep at all times, a large black iron kettle full of boiling water, hanging on the crane over the open fire. So instead of filling the can there and then she waited until Ber called, rinsed out his billy-can with boiling water, popped in two or three spoonsful of tea and handed him a piping hot can of strong brew to be sweetened to his own liking. The "road

Roadmen pose for a picture, Killeigh, 1940's. (Courtesy: John Kearney, Offaly Historical and Archaeological Society, Tullamore)

min" were all neighbours. On wet days they knew the yard gate would always be open and they were quite welcome to shelter in the barn or hayshed.

As Saint Patrick's day draws nearer the tempo of spring accelerates slightly. Pastureland grass has taken on a greener shade while violets and primroses strain for recognition along the south facing hedgerows. There is no visible stirring in the ash, beech or oak so it's too early yet to test out the old proverb, which proposed to forecast whether a dry or wet year was in the offing - "The ash before the oak, there's going to be a soak, but the oak before the ash, there will only be a splash."

The sycamores are unveiling some lively buds and tiny green leaves are peeping through on the chestnut. Velvety soft clumps of needle foliage cling like small green shuttlecocks to every branch of the larch and Matthews' field is once more a sea of yellow daffodils.

"Some early potatoes should be sown before Saint Patrick's day," was Grandad's eleventh commandment, so it's not surprising he just finished planting three short drills

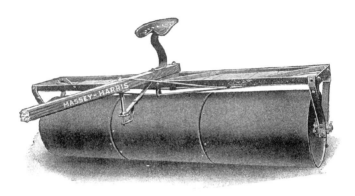

Metal Roller with seat. (Courtesy: Irish Agricultural Museum, Johnstown Castle, Wexford)

in the "ould garden". Uncle Mike, who incidentally also owns a metal roller is rolling his five acre meadow in the wood field. As cows, cattle and sheep grazed this area at different times during some autumn and winter months, rolling is now necessary to smooth off and level the animal tracks before the new meadow grows too high. The grassland beside the wood field is also a meadow, having been "let out" following a barley crop last year and Mike requested my brother Mick and I, to help him pick stones off the surface this coming Saturday. We are hoping Freddie Colton doesn't have the scutch chain-harrowed for the same day. Picking stones off the meadows to save damage to the mower blades later, was necessary in some stony fields when meadow followed a corn crop.

Tomorrow, Friday, Saint Patrick's day, a church Holy day, a National holiday and best of all for us, no school. This evening we gathered shamrock and according to Mother, the bunches we collected were a good mixture of everything that had three leaves and was green, trefoil, clover, shamrock and another unidentified item which resembled wood sorrel. However, specific plant variety never proved to be the

Chain harrow.

number one criterion in our parish when plucking shamrock for Saint Patrick's day. Size of bouquet was all important. It had to be visible from afar. It would never do if, because of its puny size, Father Kennedy failed to spot the garland on some upstanding parishioner he might encounter on his way into the vestry. While we personally did our utmost to select the genuine article, it wasn't uncommon to see well seasoned farmers sporting large ravelled tufts of young clover in their hat bands or overcoat lapels on the feast of our National Apostle. As well as the cluster of shamrock we young folk would be decked out in the morning for early Mass with "Patrick's day badges" pinned to our gansey or if the elbows were still in one piece, our school blazer. The most favoured design being a little green harp, complete with yellow strings and mounted on a background of green, white and orange ribbon. Treasured pieces indeed and the more responsible among us saved these special emblems from year to year. Unfortunately in those young days there were no Saint Patrick's day parades in country towns so the Holy day passed off quietly, even more quietly than a normal Sunday, when we might have had the opportunity to attend a parish football or hurling match in Malone's field. Much to our delight, Freddie Colton sent word to us to report for duty as soon as we got home from school on Monday, Tuesday and

Wednesday of the coming week to help him gather and burn the scutch grass.

After dinner on Saint Patrick's day a loud cheer of approval signalled the arrival of Mike Casey on his faithful Raleigh bicycle with the rusty mudguards and soft reversible saddle cover. The attractive brown saddle cover looked so inviting I always felt envious I didn't have one for my own hard leather saddle. It looked so soft and cushiony on one side and then of course could be reversed to expose the waterproof surface on rainy days. When Mike visited us on a non-working day, he enjoyed nothing better than a long relaxed ramble through every field on the farm and then finish the trip by wandering across our neighbours' turf banks on the Monettia bog which ran parallel to the south extremity of our land. Today was no exception as soon as he had a few words with Mother and asked her to have the kettle boiling when he got back, he adjusted the grey peaked cap on his head to what he referred to as the "Kildare side", and said,

"Right lads! who's for the bog?"

He didn't have to say it a second time, we jumped at the idea. Even our two dogs, Pip the little white mongrel with the brown patch on his ear, and Jess the Irish wheaten terrier, frisked and barked in agreement. On walks like this we often picked up little gems of information and Mike engendered in us a strong love and respect for nature and all that goes with the great outdoors. He remarked on the patchy green haze of embryo leaves which were now beginning to appear here and there in the hawthorn hedge, or whitethorn as we called it. He pointed out their evident contrast to the blackthorn bushes which still had developed little or no leaves, despite the fact that they had already produced small white blossoms. He told us the sloe, the fruit of the blackthorn was the forerunner of practically every variety of cultivated plum and showed us how to make a whistle from a short length of young ash sapling.

While passing through the ould house field and Roberts field, he pointed out the tall stately beech trees and the majestic oaks which we were privileged to have and asked us to make sure, as we grew up, to keep the parasite ivy cut from their trunks. In the well field there were a few young furze or gorse bushes springing up in various places. He suggested these shrubs would increase and multiply quickly and once established would be difficult to eradicate. He went on to explain, in his young days, he and his brothers had to reclaim two or three acres of moorland which were over-run with furze bushes. The process was known as "stubbin' furze". First of all the tops were cut off four or five inches above the ground, left for a few days to die then burned in heaps. A pick and a mattock, commonly called a mallet in the midlands, were used to dig up and hack out every vestige of the remaining root. According to our uncle

this was an energy-sapping task if the roots were deep, so he advised us to get working on the young growths before they became established.

"And talkin' about work", said Mike, "I'll be ready to sow me spuds in about ten days time, and I

The curlew.

119

want a couple o' you buckos to plant seed."

We knew there was only one answer to that question, because we needed him to till and make ready for our own crop, soon after he had finished his.

"That suits us fine", said Christy, "we're givin' three evenin's to Freddie Colton next week, Monday, Tuesday and Wednesday."

"Well, ye can do Thursday and Friday for Freddie as well, if ye like", said Mike, "meself and Ned will be harrowin', openin' drills and puttin' out dung all next week." He continued, "We'll have the seed-sower in action early the followin' week, sowin' a lock o' spring whate, an' then start on the spuds on Friday."

"We might take Friday off from school", said I hopefully, "then we could do Friday and Saturday with you."

"That's what I'd be hopin' for", said Mike, "I always aim to get the spuds in durin' the first few days of April."

The walk across the bog proved to be as interesting and as enjoyable as our farm stroll. In the distance a group of five curlews took turns piping out their long, poignant notes, slow at first then speeding up and rising in pitch to their characteristic flourish at the end. For some reason I always felt that this clear, distinctive call of the curlew had some inbuilt strains of melancholy.

"That's a sure sign o' rain when ye hear the curlews cryin' like that." said Mike.

To us, the few clouds in the sky were high and did not look at all menacing. The breeze came from the south-east, not a usual point for rain according to Grandad. However, we didn't dispute uncle Mike's theory, he had been around for much longer than us and generally came up right about most other things. In a quick flurry behind us my

120

brother Mick ran down the high bank and jumped over one of last year's bog holes on to the low bank. He looked up at us and challenged,

"Come on! I jumped to there," as he marked a certain point in the turf mould, with his boot, "Can any o' ye bate that?"

"Well, ye can forget about me," grinned uncle Mike, "I'm too young for that sort o' caper; and you're too young too," he said in a more serious note turning to our youngest brother Tim who wasn't yet six years old and taking him by the hand warned, "don't dare try anythin' like that or we'll be fishin' ye out o' five feet o' bog water."

Christy and I had a go and out-did each other by a few inches as well as overhauling Mick's leap. However, this was no great surprise, we had practiced the routine earlier in the year and the variation in distance leaped, worked out to be in direct proportion to the variance in age. I bettered Christy by a few degrees and Christy out-jumped Mick by a similar margin. Uncle Mike and Tim made their way carefully down from the high bank to join the long jumpers on the low bank and reminded us it was time we headed back home. As we tramped along the narrow heathery path across the remaining allotments towards the bog lane, which led to the main road, Mike spotted in the distance a clump of long stemmed heather.

"Run over there and pull a handful o' that for a besom for yer mother," he suggested. As I approached the cluster of rich tall heather, two red grouse exploded into the air with whirring wing beats and quickly disappeared beyond the skyline over the high bank.

"Maybe they were makin' a nest," queried Mick.

"Well have a look and see for yourself, when ye're

pullin' the besom," suggested Mike.

The two of us examined the area carefully as we pulled the tall strands of heather, but found no sign of nest building.

"Did ye know that grouse look back in flight when they're flushed out like that?" said Mike.

"Ah! pull the other one," said I holding out my left leg in front of him.

"No, I'm dead serious," he continued, "a red grouse is one of the few birds that look back in flight after been roused. Next time ye rise one, just take a closer look."

Wednesday evening Christy and I completed the scutch picking task for Freddie Colton and collected three shillings each. This was more than we expected, we had calculated three half days at one and threepence a day would realise about one and tenpence or one and elevenpence.

"Ah! ye were well worth it," said Freddie, "sure ye worked much later aich evenin' than I did myself."

Well, whether we were worth it or not, the three shillings looked good to us. Unless Mother was having another cash flow problem, I might be able to hold on and get a new tyre for my bike and Christy had long promised to buy a new cover for the football with the next money he got his hands on.

As the days passed and the evenings grew a little longer, news came through that Mike Casey was ready and had the seed all cut in preparation for the potato sowing. Traditionally this seed cutting job fell to the woman of the house but as Mike and his two brothers Tom and Ned were bachelors, there was no woman of the house. Their mother, Grannie Casey, now a widow for some considerable number of years, reckoned she had enough to do without the added burden of cutting seed. So each year the responsibility was left in the capable hands of Tom and he considered himself to be an expert at the craft.

"Ye've got to choose yer potatoes well," he said to us one year while sorting seed at our house.

The normal practice was to sort seed into three or four sacks at the pit, before cutting and indeed this often proved to be a very cold station, sitting at a potato pit all muffled up in top-coat and hat in bitter March weather.

"Ye have to pick them not too big and not too small, an' as ye split them make sure there's two or three eyes in aich section," said Tom.   "That size o' potato you'd split in two and that size would give ye three seed," he continued, as he held up two varying sizes of Up-to-dates.   "When yer cuttin' a spud to give three seeds, ye cut about a third off and then split the remaining bigger piece at right angles to the first cut. An' finally ye could plant that size o' potato as it is without splittin' it at all," he said as he showed us another one of smaller dimension.

"Pierce" seed sower. (Courtesy: Wexford County Library)

During the days Tom spent cutting seed Uncle Mike came to us to sow the remainder of our wheat and barley crops with his Pierce seedsower. He knew it would have to be a concerted effort and worked late into the evenings. At the end of his labour we had four acres of wheat sown in Roberts' field, three in the Long field and four acres of barley between Murrays' field and Martins' field. Before leaving he promised mother to sow the oats in the Turn field the first opportunity he got but right now he had to finish sowing his own spring wheat.

On Thursday after school I cycled down to Killeenmore to follow the seedsower with Mike for a few bouts, making sure I gave myself enough time to get back home before dark. Because of other special chores which I had to complete, I didn't really get a chance to see the seedsower in operation when he was sowing our own crops. As with the reaper and binder and the hay-lifter, I had a special fascination for the seedsower. It had two huge wheels, bigger than the wheels on Jack McDonalds sidecar. The broad rectangular feed-box, suitably designed wide at the top and narrowing almost to a point at the bottom, held the seed wheat. Running across inside the base of the feed-box were a series of small cog wheels mounted on a metal drive shaft. These forced the grain down the chutes to the spring-loaded sowing modules or sowing arms which penetrated two or three inches into the soil.

Periodically and particularly on the headlands, I noticed uncle Mike opened the lid of the feed-box and glanced in. On one occasion I managed to peep in too and could see the grain appeared to be stained a muddy blue. He informed me this was a special seed dressing to eliminate certain crop diseases later on during the growing season. He also told me that by glancing into the box he could check if the grain continued to feed down at the same uniform rate right across the box, and if not he could then investigate and check for a blocked outlet. Before I left for home I had to give Mike the bad news that we could not get permission to stay home from school the next day, Friday, to start planting his potatoes. He was very disappointed and barked,

"Why the hell didn't ye tell me earlier, it's too late to look for help now."

He then cooled down a bit and decided he wouldn't start until Saturday, hoping he'd have time to organise some local lads to carry on on Monday.

8   Planting the spuds

Saturday morning the first day of April dawned cool and dry and after an early breakfast the three of us set out on our bicycles for Killeenmore. I had my own bike, Christy used Mother's "ould spudler", as she called it and Mick succeeded in getting a loan of eldest sister Mary's second hand semi-sports for the day. After parking our three mounts in the barn Grannie met us and insisted we'd have to have "a cup o' hot tay before goin' out on a cowld mornin' like that". Obviously she overlooked the fact that we had already been out and cycled almost three miles, part of the way, against a south east breeze. However, we didn't object and before you could say, "new potatoes!" had executed a quick disappearing trick on three mugs of tea and six slices of her white soda bread.

During this time Mike and Tom had yoked one of the black draught horses to the cart and loaded three sacks of artificial fertiliser, four sacks of seed potatoes and three praisceens. Tom then sat up on the slat of the cart and drove out to the headland of the potato field while the rest of us walked behind. The field was no more than one hundred yards from the dwelling house. As Tom journeyed along he shouted back to us, "have you gang o' school-goers heard about this new type o' seed potato they have developed in Germany?"

"No! begorrah we haven't", said Christy, "where did ye hear about it, or what's new about it?"

"Well, accordin' to what I read, it grows and blossoms in four weeks after sowin', and then ye can dig the new potatoes two weeks after that agin."

"Pierce" moulding plough. (Courtesy: Wexford County Library)

"That sounds impossible," I piped in, "No plant could blossom in four weeks after sowin'."

"Well, there y'are," said Tom, "that's what I read in black and white in the "Irelands Own.""

At that point Uncle Mike started giggling.

"He didn't read it in the "Irelands Own," Mike laughed, "I read that magazine every week and I saw nothin' in it about a new German spud."

As Mike continued laughing he blurted out, "ah! now I know what yer man's at, he's tryin' to make an April fool o' ye."

Not until then did it dawn on us, that the first day of April had indeed arrived. As Mick shouted back to Tom, "now aren't ye the smart one, with yer April fool at this hour o' the mornin' ," the three of us vowed we would pay him back dearly before the day was out.

Mike Casey had a reputation as a good ploughman and had won a few minor prizes in local ploughing championships, but here in this field, it became obvious he was equally at home with the moulding plough. The drills were perfectly uniform and each one as straight as the barrel of a gun. Tom had now been joined by his brother Ned and they assisted each other in lifting down a sack of seed potatoes and a sack of fertiliser from the cart, leaving both on the headland. They then drove about half way up the drills, dropped off a second sack of seed potatoes and proceeded to the far headland where they unloaded a third, together with a further supply of fertiliser.

The farmyard manure which Mike and Ned had put out the previous day lay distributed in small piles along the top of each drill no more than a few yards apart.

"How the hell can anyone open drills as straight as that with a pair o' horses?" asked Christy.

"Awe, you could do it too, if ye were at it as long as me," said Mike, dismissively.

"Begorrah, I have me doubts about that," answered Christy, as he and Mick started to fill their praisceens with seed potatoes from one of the sacks on the headland.

The praisceen when in working position looked like a rough brown apron hanging to one side of the wearer over the shoulder. It was made from an empty bran or pollard sack, slit down one side and across the bottom to give a single oblong piece. A further slit going more than quarter way down through the sacking, was then made from the centre of one of the shorter sides. The resultant two loose corners were then tied together and the seed planter slipped his head and right arm through the slit, so that one side of the praisceen passed over his left shoulder and the other underneath his right arm. The action of taking up the remaining two corners and holding them together in the left hand, formed a deep pouch capable of holding almost two stones of seed.

Needless to say we never filled our praisceens to that extent but we did know that older and stronger lads like Mick Dolan and Paddy Clear often carried two stones at a time.

"Right lads!" shouted uncle Mike, "we're scratchin'

around long enough, we'll make a start in the name o' God. You plant the first drill, Christy and Ned'll put in after ye, an' Mick can take the second with you puttin' in", he said motioning to me.

Puttin' in, of course meant using a light four-grained fork to spread the farmyard manure over the newly planted seed.

"Yer smart uncle Tom will folly the both o' ye, shakin' in the artificial fertiliser," Mike continued.

There were few clouds in the sky and the morning turned out to be bright and dry with even a hint of warmth flowing from the April sun. The soil in the newly opened drills felt soft and yielding, so before depositing the first seed the two planters, Christy and Mick, decided to slip off their boots and stockings and savour the texture of the soft malleable earth as it pressed up between their toes. From the end of April onwards we normally went to school in our bare feet as did ninety per cent of the pupils of Killurin and Killeigh National schools. Taking off the boots for the first time in April, gave a great feeling of freedom and agility. Very often the first day planting seed heralded the first day in bare feet so it was no surprise that the two lads decided to make their debut at this time and discard the hob nails.

Christy and Mick went off at a steady pace, holding the praisceen in the left hand, taking out fistfuls of seed with the right and placing them in the alley approximately ten inches apart while shuffling backwards all the time. There is no doubt planters had a special controlled talent, performed in perfect rhythm as they reversed up the drill with right foot slightly ahead of the left, then in a semi-erect position, dipping the right hand into the praisceen before bending or stooping to deftly place the cut tubers, equidistant from each other in the alley.

With sacks of seed on both headlands and one in the centre of the field, the two planters never had too far to walk to replenish their supplies as the praisceens became empty. After some two hours they had made good headway and were several drills ahead of Ned Casey and I who were of course "puttin in." Uncle Mike by this time had driven the horse and cart back to the barn in the farmyard to collect further sacks of seed potatoes and fertiliser and was now helping us to make up some of the leeway with the planters.

Just on the stroke of eleven Grannie came into view on the near headland carrying a gallon of tea in one hand and a black oilcloth shopping bag, which had seen better days, in the other. She didn't have to call us. We had been scanning the horizon in that direction for some time in anticipation of her arrival. As soon as we saw her we swiftly dropped tools and praisceens and made our way down to meet her. Grannie was an ould-timer of rare quality, a strict hardy old lady who could spot or generate in her own imagination a danger point in every action, deed or performance which children might undertake.

"What are you two fellas doin' in yer bare feet?" she rasped in a stern voice to Christy and Mick, as she steadied the gallon of tea on a level patch of grass, and took a handful of mugs and a brown paper parcel from the shopping bag. "If ye get a cowld, yer mother'll be blamin' me," she continued.

"Sure we go to school in our bare feet, Grannie," answered Christy", an' we'll be in our bare feet from now 'til next September," he added.

"Well, I don't mind June or July for bare feet but April or May is far too early. Did yer mother never tell ye

130

the ould proverb, "Cast not a clout 'til May is out," she said in a more conciliatory voice. Then with a swirl of her long black skirt she slowly eased herself on to her knees, at the same time arranging an empty sack as a cushion against the damp grass. It became obvious from her facial expression that she was now more at peace with herself, having aired her opinions about bare feet in the chilly months of spring. At least if we got a cold now she could always say, "well, I towld ye so, but ye wouldn't heed me warnin'."

From her kneeling position she handed out mugs of tea to eagerly outstretched hands while uncle Mike opened the brown paper parcel and distributed thick slices of loaf bread covered in butter and apricot jam. This welcome break which helped to alleviate the strain on some aching backs, while at the same time ease the hunger pains also gave us an opportunity to carry out a few running repairs on ourselves. I had to journey back to the house with Grannie when she returned, to pick up a strip of adhesive dressing for a burst blister on the palm of my hand caused by the rough handle of the four-grained fork I was using. Christy prevailed upon Ned Casey to remove a fragment of potato from underneath a finger nail, a common hazard experienced by many potato planters and often proved painful unless the foreign body was removed quickly.

Four o' clock in the afternoon heralded a welcome repetition of the eleven o' clock morning break. The only difference this time, we got tea and rhubarb cake. The rhubarb cake, not rhubarb tart, like mother's apple cake, was a Grannie speciality with its deep, pliable, brown sticky crusts cradling so many soft chunks of succulent rhubarb.

"Ate it up quickly and don't be lettin' that good rich juice run down yer fingers," she said to Mick, the youngest worker in the gang.

During the working week uncle Mike spent most of his time in a rush, so it surprised nobody that he finished first. He emptied the remnants of his tea mug into the hedge, lit a cigarette and advised all and sundry he was off to "get the horses and start closin' a few drills". This again called for the two-winged moulding plough, which together with the swingletrees had been left on the headland in the shelter of an oak tree since the drills were opened. Very soon Mike arrived back leading his two black horses completely harnessed with winkers, reins, collar, hames, drumaun and draught chains. He yoked his willing team to the moulding plough, joining each pair of draught chains by hook to their respective swingletrees and linking them in turn to the main swingletree or butt swing as we called it, which he attached to the plough.

With much interest we watched him manoeuvre the horses gently getting the plough in position, its soleplate and nib or sock dipping low into the centre of the first drill. With a friendly "glick, glick, hup, hup," the team moved forward and the two wings of the plough split the drill, moulding one half of the friable crumbly soil in over the manure-covered seed in the left alley and the other half, over the manure-covered seed in the alley to the right. On the return run the plough repeated the operation on the next drill, and that of course resulted in the formation of the first new closed drill of potatoes. Then each subsequent journey in either direction, completed another fully formed drill.

Uncle Mike understood we did not dare stay away from school the following week, so he accepted he would have to finish the potato sowing with his brothers together with the local help he had been promised from Peter Gallagher and John Conroy. Despite the fact that we let him down, he nevertheless promised he and Tom would be coming to our house "at the tail end o' next week" to give us a hand sowing our crop. Sunday and Monday proved to be two bitter cold days with the wind moving from south east to east. They certainly weren't days for bare feet and we were glad to revert to boots and stockings once more.

"Ye know there's a blow o' snow in that wind," said Grandad, "yer uncle Mike was lucky to get so much done in the last few days."

"Sure what else could ye expect durin' the three borried days," answered Mother, and then nodding her head towards us, "an' to think these gombeens were plantin' seed in their bare feet on Saturday."

"Sure it was warm on Saturday Mammie," we all chimed in, "an the clay was gorgeous and soft on our feet."

"Well, yer Grannie should have had more sense than lettin' ye take off yer boots durin' the three borried days."

We had often heard the legend of "the three borried days" before. Apparently, as the story goes, An Bo Riabhach" the brindled cow or sometimes just the ould cow constantly complained to all her friends of how cruel March weather was with its east wind, hail, snow and gales. March became very annoyed and promised it would teach the "ould cow" a lesson and blow severe weather until it destroyed her. By the end of the month it hadn't succeeded and decided to borrow three days from April, with much more severe conditions to finish off the job. So the first three days of April are traditionally expected to be very cold and harsh and in the midlands, at least, were known as the three borried days.

Very often indeed, as was the case with the second two days of April this year, the legend proved uncannily true and even in years when the early April climate was unquestionably mild Mother would not compromise the accuracy of the story.

"I know the sun is shining and the breeze is from the south but it's still the "borried" days an' ye shouldn't take off that woolly gansey," she might say to one of us, as we tried to come to terms with the temperature of a warm introduction to this capricious month. However, this year we needed no warnings to leave on our ganseys, boots or stockings. Mother and Grandad were always wary of east wind and told us on many occasions that in early springtime, it was "good for neither man or beast."

Luckily the borried days receded just as fast as they

Mrs. Carolan's Shop at Gorteen Bridge, formerly a forge. The shop is currently owned by Mrs. Lena Casey.

The Skylark.

arrived. By Good Friday, the seventh of the month, the wind had veered around to an almost southerly direction and the weather looked good for Easter. With all the fasting and abstinence during Lent we succeeded in saving up a few shillings pocket money and eagerly looked forward to visiting Mrs. Carolan's shop at Gorteen bridge. We knew exactly what we wanted, having picked out the items in the window several times over the past days on our way home from school. Top of the list of course was a Mickey Mouse square, then a few specialities like cocoa-nut biscuits and Easter eggs with white and yellow chocolate mousse inside. The weather on Easter Sunday lived up to expectations, a nice bright day with a warm southerly breeze. Most of the family went to early Mass and of course Mary being the most observant of us all, enthused to Mother when she came home, about the little blobs of green, blue and yellow sunlight which she saw dancing through the stained glass window high up on the opposite wall of the church.

"An' what's strange about that?" asked Mother, "don't ye know the sun always dances on Easter morning."

The following days up to mid-month produced typical seasonal weather. Soft April showers and warm April sun transformed the once brown tilled fields along the road to school into square and oblong lakes of spring green, as the newly emerged tiny grain stalks rippled, and struggled against the southerly breeze. The flutter and roll of the little

135

swaying blades, suggested movement like surface water as the currents of air whipped across them in waves. Hedgerows were aglow with primrose, violet and cowslip while fledgeling grasses in every new meadow tried desperately to overhaul the spurting daisy. The low area of Monettia bog looked magnificent in its blazing yellow mantle of golden furze bushes, broken only by the emerging purple blossom of the heather. Along the slopes of the Slieve Bloom the tall pine and Scot's fir appeared to be standing on a green and white carpet, fashioned by the tiny flowers of the wood sorrel. The arrival of these warm April days coaxed out that little red and black spotted insect and gardener's friend, the ladybird. Hedgehogs and squirrels had long since departed their hibernation abodes and the cheering song of the skylark filled the air every day. How beautifully the scene was captured by the poet, Percy Bysshe Shelley:-

Hail to thee blithe spirit, bird thou never wert,
That from heaven or near it, pourest thy full heart
In profuse strains of un-premeditated art.
Higher still and higher from the earth thou springest,
Like a cloud of fire; the blue deep thou wingest,
And singing still dost soar, and soaring ever singest.

(From "Ode to a Skylark", by Percy Bysshe Shelley)

Most farmers are now well ahead with spring sowing. In many cases all potato and grain crops are in. On the way home from school yesterday, we stopped to see Johnny Walsh sowing mangolds. The ground preparation for this root crop corresponded exactly with that for potatoes. Usually stubble from the previous year's grain harvest, it was ploughed and tilled, drills were opened with the moulding plough and farmyard manure put in. The drills were then closed and left ready for sowing. The sowing implement was known as a turnip barrow, although also used when sowing beet or mangold seed. It could be pulled by one horse or for that matter by a pony. A simple piece of equipment with an hour-glass roller in front which when in motion flattened down the crest of the drill being sown. Mounted behind this roller lay a round saucepan-like seed box with a revolving set of three or four small brushes positioned inside the base of the box. The brushes were driven by a connecting rod from the front roller and they forced the seed down a narrow metal chute which penetrated about two inches into the flattened soil. Situated behind the chute, a second roller closed the earth in over the seed in the track made by the metal chute and re-flattened the drill.

"An' how many slaps did ye get from Mr. Hutton, today, lads?" said Johnny when he saw us on the headland.

'Sure we never get slaps, Johnny," answered Christy,

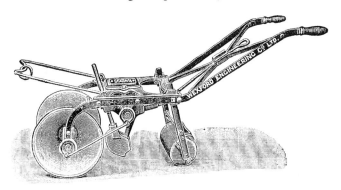

Turnip barrow. Used for sowing turnip, mangold or beet seed.
(Courtesy: Irish Agricultural Museum, Johnstown Castle, Wexford)

with emphasis on the word we. "We always know our lessons."

"Well then I'll axe ye a question, an' I'll see how good ye are," Johnny continued. "What are them small birds flyin' up high over there in the direction o' that beech tree?"

"Be Japers! they're swallows," I exclaimed in excitement, "an' they're the first swallows I saw this year."

"Begob, ye're spot on," agreed Johnny, "they're swallows alright, but can ye tell me what does that mane?"

"I suppose when we see swallows flyin' high, it means more good weather," volunteered Christy.

"Well, begob I can't dispute that, a-tana-rate, but that's not exactly what I was gettin' at."

"I think ye'll have to tell us what ye were gettin' at so, Johnny," said Mick.

"Ah, ye're no good, ye're only howldin' me up from sowin' this lock o' mangolds," he replied, " I'll have to answer the question meself. When ye see the first swallows o' the year, that's the sign that spring has officially arrived for the farmer. Ye can forget about these yarns regarding La Fheile Bhride being the first o' spring, that's only accordin' to the calendar."

Then with a flourish and a few quick tugs on the reins, he steered his brown mare and the turnip barrow on to the next drill. When we arrived home we told Mother the story about our encounter with Johnny.

"Aye, some people say spring truly arrives with the first swallows," she agreed, "but they have different signs in different parts o' the country, an' different still in England." She continued, "Ould Frank Kelly when he was young worked on a farm in Lincolnshire, in England. He towld me the farmers there, had a sayin' that — — —". At this point she

Cutting Turf.

did her best to stifle a giggle, —- "that spring arrived when ye could sit on fresh soil with yer bare backside without feelin' the cowld." As she finished she burst into a hearty laugh and at the same time hid her mouth with her hand as if she felt she had gone outside the bounds of good taste by using the word backside. Of course we did indeed think it funny to hear Mother using that word in an amusing sense and then giggling with embarrassment. We had often heard it on other occasions when she was in a bad mood over some of our indiscretions and threatening us with "a few belts of the strap across the backside."

In the open spaces of pasture and moorland, starlings hop around in pairs picking up traineens, straws and grasses to use as nest building material in the crevice of some wall or tree hollow. The magpie too, which most farmers looked on as vermin is collecting sticks and twigs to construct or more accurately throw together that gangly mound which suffices as a nest. Generally unpopular, it has a reputation for stealing hen eggs and other smaller birds eggs. Mike Casey told us that once in his schoolboy days he took eggs from a magpie's nest, boiled them and then replaced them when they cooled

Wheeling turf to drier ground.

off to watch the female sit hatching for weeks and weeks before eventually giving it up as a bad job. In the nearby pines or Scot's fir, the coal tit pipes out its two-bar melody in surprisingly strong decibels for such a small bird, telling us that summer is on the way. We are now well into the third week of April and whatever about the pros and cons regarding swallows being the harbingers of spring, there appeared nothing in the full nature calendar of the year which affected me more profoundly than the first call of the cuckoo.

The Cuckoo.

No doubt this had an uplifting effect on many other people too, but in my case, the first sound of the cuckoo always filled me with a surge of pure excitement bordering on ecstasy. Even to the present day I find it hard to explain but, hearing the first calls of this most welcome visitor, fills me with an emotional delight.   Standing in a meadow, on a bog or on a hilltop, listening to the cuckoo's song I still repeat over and over again that most discerning observation of Michael Bruce:-

"There is no sorrow in thy song, no winter in thy year."

From our early childhood we always knew when to expect the arrival of the first cuckoo because we eagerly learned this special little rhyme from our mother:-

> In April she comes
> In May she sings all day
> In June she changes her tune
> In July away she'll fly
> In August go she must.

We also learned something about this spring visitor and her behaviour from another little verse we picked up from uncle Mike:-

> The cuckoo's a small bird, she sings as she flies,
> She brings us good tidings and tells us no lies,
> She feeds on the small birds to keep her voice clear,
> And the more she cries cuckoo, the summer draws near.

A very welcome visitor but unfortunately with some strange selfish traits of character. As most people know the cuckoo never builds her own nest but lays eggs in what we term the "host nest." One of the most popular of these being the meadow pipit whose eggs like the cuckoo's are a speckled greyish brown, though somewhat smaller. The hedge sparrow too is a much favoured host despite the fact that there is no similarity in the egg colour. Other hosts include the robin and wagtail. As soon as the young cuckoo is hatched, it pushes out the other chicks over the side of the nest thus ensuring that all food morsels are fed to it. However, I personally can make allowances for all these short-comings and I still remember so well, she always did indeed arrive in April and sang loud and clear each day until that strange break in her voice, between mid and end June. Then as she prepared to depart our shores and fly south to a warmer climate all sadly fell silent until her inspiring return in the spring of the following year.

Though April showers constituted a common feature during the remaining days of the month they were intermingled with good stretches of warm sunshine. Tadpoles became evident in the overflow pool beside Mac's well on the way from school and in the drinking pond in "Clooney's field", where we did our winter skating. Wild strawberry plants were straining through the grassy undergrowth along the south facing hedgerows and the odd butterfly displayed its new spring colour scheme.

9   The May Bush

May day dawned bright and cool. The high rolling clouds seemed to tell us that April had failed to deliver her full allocation of showers.

"The weather's not up yit," remarked Grandad as he glanced at mother fixing coloured ribbons, bunches of primroses and daisies, egg shells and short strips of tinsel or silver cigarette paper on the whitethorn cutting which would serve as this year's May bush. When she finished the titivating, Grandad brought it out to the back yard and firmly installed it in its usual position from where it could be seen from the road and would proudly remain there for the thirty one days of May. The origin of the May bush is not too clear. Some sources suggest it is a relic of an old pagan practice which has survived through the ages. Nevertheless, every household in the parish decorated and displayed a May bush. It was accepted as an omen of good luck and bestowed protection on the complete homestead, animals, crops, fowl and pets. The usual theory put forward for the use of egg shells as decorations is the fact that eggs would have been a popular food item during the season of Lent and the shells were saved for later use on the May bush.

Gathering bunches of the beautiful white mayflower from the hedgerows to decorate little altars in honour of Our Lady, was another favoured practice in the parish. Although we all helped to collect the flowers, it fell to Mary and Margaret, ably assisted by Mother to decorate and adorn our floral offering to the Blessed Virgin. For the grown-ups including our uncles Mike, Tom and Ned the maypole dancing at Durrow, just north of Tullamore, was in full swing every Sunday night throughout the month.

After Mass on Sunday myself and youngest brother Tim, who would be six years old in a few days time, collected some clusters of cowslips and I showed him how to make dodge balls. Making dodge balls developed into a favourite pastime with many schoolgoers at this time of the year. Handfuls of cowslips were gathered, the multi-blossomed heads were then cut off from the stems and hung flowers downward on a length of strong twine, getting as many heads as possible on the string. Then as the twine was tightly knotted the cowslips were drawn together into a round ball formation. Second and third knots were added and the two fly ends of the twine cut off leaving a perfectly formed ball of flowers. The soft ball proved a great attraction for young children to throw, catch or kick without any real exposure to hurt or injury and of course they got endless satisfaction in assembling it. Mary and Margaret preferred making daisy chains, sometimes using small daisies and on other occasions working with the larger dog-daisy. Needless to say the chains and necklaces had a short life span, but certainly gave a measure of achievement and enjoyment in carefully slitting each stem and seeing the chain grow, adding flower after flower.

Unfortunately the newspapers each week carried a lot of speculation about war. Uncle Mike told us that young men in Britain were being conscripted into the armed forces. He told us Mr. De Valera was pursuing a policy of neutrality for Ireland and objected strongly to conscription being implemented in Northern Ireland. Nevertheless, the Prime Minister of Northern Ireland, Mr. Craigavon, insisted that Northern Ireland formed part of the British empire and they were ready to do their bit. Seeing that a section of Ireland was involved we became worried and carefully followed the news items each week in the "Offaly Independent." As the days passed we were delighted to read that Mr. De Valera had visited the United States to enlist American support for his objection and then shortly afterwards heard Mr. Chamberlain, the British Prime Minister, had announced there would be no conscription in Northern Ireland.

In contrast, out in the fields, bird nesting time was now really in full swing. Between the three of us, Christy, Mick and myself, we had already found a chaffinch nest and a thrush's nest in the whitethorn ditch in Martins field, a blackbird's in the laurel hedge in Grannie's and two robins' nests in the low bank near the well. Beech, oak, sycamore and birch are draped in overcoats of various shades of green while the chestnut hangs out its mass of white candelabra clusters on every branch. As far as the eye can see across the broad expanse of cut-away bog the furze bushes are aflame in an abundance of golden yellow blooms. The row of apple trees beside the dwelling house, and all the fruit trees in the ould garden are resplendent in a blanket of pink appleblossom. The little white flowers of the hawthorn, so abundant in every hedgerow, gives one the feeling there has been an early May snowfall.

> Among the many buds proclaiming May
> Decking the fields in holiday array,
> Striving who shall surpass in braverie;
> Marke the faire flowering of the hawthorn tree
> Who finely clothed in a robe of white
> Fills full the wanton eye with May's delight.

Chaucer.

Drill saddle harrow. (Courtesy: Department of Irish Folklore, University College, Dublin)

So far the first half of May has been reasonably dry and the threatened backlog of April showers never materialised. The cuckoo now sings all day long from early morning, sometimes even wakening us at four thirty or five a.m. as she pipes her two-note melody from the topmost branch of the chestnut tree in the haggard. Grandad looks out across Fletcher's field watching Joe Fletcher saddle-harrowing his early potato crop. The saddle-harrow, a light wooden implement, arched to suit the contour of the drill, was effectively used to remove early weeds and this loosening of the soil facilitated growth of the seed potato. All of a sudden a sidhe gaoith or fairy wind appeared from nowhere whipping up leaves, twigs and dust from the dry earth as it weaved and swerved across the drills, then disappeared just as quickly through the hedge into Elliot's field. This phenomenon of course was one of those whirlwinds which usually occur on warm days in late spring or early summer. They are caused by the spiral rising of an overheated layer of air near the ground. The old folk always referred to them as fairy winds.

"What causes the sidhe gaoith?" we asked Grandad, "or where does it come from?"

"That's the fairies or the good people gallopin' past on their little mounts. O' course bein' fairies ye can't see them, ye can only see the dust kicked up by the hooves o' their small ponies," he answered. "It's always considered lucky to see a fairy wind," he continued, "an' it's supposed to be a sign o' fine weather."

"Well, that's a pity," said mother, "we could well do with a few good showers o' rain for the corn crops."

"Ah! well sure these ould sayin's are not always right," replied Grandad hopefully, "maybe we will get a shower or two in the next few days."

Showers of rain or wet weather were the last things in the world that the young folk wanted. Kellys' field was nice and firm now and in great shape for our hurling practices, it could deliver a good bounce in the ball if we changed over to playing football. The narrow path through the furze bushes to the Glosh which we used when going to catch pinkeens was no longer mucky and the road to school dry and dusty and warm on the feet. However, much to our disgust, within a day or two Mother's dreams were realised. Thick, dark grey clouds rolled in from the south west over the Slieve Blooms, and it rained almost non-stop on Friday from mid-day to bed time. It rained so heavily Mother had to yoke Kerry the red pony and drive up to the "ould house" near McDonald's to pick us up from school. She brought hats, raincoats and best of all, dry sacks which we wrapped around our legs and thighs as we nestled down in the straw in the cart. Much to their delight we managed to fit in Con and Charlie Kelly who lived near us and gave them a lift as well.

The heavy fall of rain made the ground soft and with good intervals of sunshine during the following days, the extra spurt of growth in the wheat and barley fields became really noticeable. But, if it did, so did the growth of young thistles in all the corn crops. These intruders were not at all acceptable or tolerated by any farmer and of course all land owners knew they could be prosecuted under some Noxious Weed Act if thistles, docks and such like were not kept under control. At harvest time nothing could be more irritating or sore on the hands than trying to manipulate sheaves of wheat, oats or barley which had an abundance of dead thistle thorns when stooking, stacking or later on making the rick. The dead thorn seemed to be far more vicious than the live one on the thistle in its growing state. Now was the right time of the year to rid the corn crops of this scourge. We got our instructions from Mother.

"For the next week I want ye to specially hurry home early from school and help Grandad to pull thistles in all the corn fields. If ye don't get the job finished, ye'll have to spend all day Saturday at it as well and forget about hurlin' ."

"Forgettin' about hurlin' " was pretty rough but we had encountered this type of disappointment before and knew we had no way out. However, to us, thistle pulling wasn't as hard a task as plantin' seed or pickin' potatoes and with the soft ground we even

Thistle puller.

148

experienced an element of satisfaction, in seeing the long white root slip through the yielding soil.

The implement we used was aptly named a thistle puller, hand operated, a scissors style instrument with two long handles. When closed together they activated a metal pincer-like head with two probing mandibles similar to a duck's bill. By operating the wooden handles the duck's bill opened and we pushed it down into the earth with one probe on either side of the thistle root. The handles were then closed together and the offending weed steadily removed like a bad tooth. If we uprooted some young grain stalks in the process we dropped them back in position, pressed down the earth and proceeded to the next pull. Grandad, in his own deliberate way, worked very hard during the days while we were at school and we laboured long and late in the evenings. Our strenuous efforts proved worthwhile. We succeeded in completing the task by mid-morning on Saturday and that of course meant we were free for the hurling match on Saturday evening, although our arms were pretty tired and stiff.

There was now a genuine warmth in the air as the weather improved daily. The oak, beech and chestnut draped the countryside in their magnificent shades of green. These were contrasted elegantly by the great artist of nature, with the purple of the lilac, the pure white of the hawthorn and the

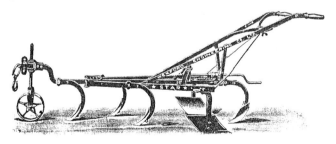

Drill grub. (Courtesy: Wexford County Library)

light pink of the crabapple buds. All root crop fields were alive with activity. Pat Purcell, wearing a straw hat for the first time this year and with the sleeves of his blue striped shirt rolled up above the elbows, seemed to be in total harmony with his following of crows as he drill grubbed his beet. This operation to remove all weeds from the alleys called into use the drill grub pulled by one horse. The two groups of three curved tines arranged in staggered formation on either side of the implement, guaranteed that no area of soil remained unturned. This grubbing operation would be carried out again in a few weeks time just before thinning the beet. The second run had a two-fold benefit. It again uprooted the new growth of weeds and at the same time left the soil in the alleys, soft and flexible on the knees of the thinners.

In a field not far away, Jim Connolly rolled a four acre crop of barley with his metal roller.

"It helps to firm up the clay around the roots," said Jim, "and push down into the soil any loose stones that might cause problems for the cutting blades of the reaper-and-binder at harvest time."

Nearby, on his own farm Con Kelly was lettin' out a field of oats. Lettin' out meant sowing hay seeds in the already growing corn crop. The theory being, by the time the

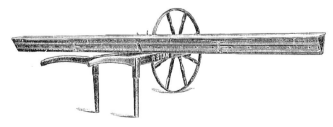

Hay seed barrow(Courtesy:
Irish Agricultural Museum, Johnstown Castle, Wexford)

hay seeds sprouted and started growing, the oat stalks would be well developed and accordingly stifle the growth of the meadow for that year. At harvest time this grass showed up as a "good butt" in the sheaves. The following year then, the field would not be ploughed or tilled and consequently the new meadow flourished. The hay seed, a mixture of Timothy, Italian ryegrass, meadow fescue, clover and maybe some other variety was sown with a hayseed barrow. This hand operated apparatus needed no horse power, it was propelled forward manually just like a hand-cart. Con wheeled the light wooden barrow with its large wheel and the long seed box, which extended six or seven feet out over each side of the barrow. The seed box, as in the case of the seed-sower already described, had a series of brushes inside which revolved and forced the small seeds out through a row of apertures set a few inches apart, right across its full width. The brushes were activated by a drive shaft from the ground wheel. After sowing Con rolled the crop to embed the newly fallen hay seeds into the soil. Right along the valley landscape, men in shirt sleeves could be seen deploying single horses or following teams of two while others were shaking manure, spreading top-dressing or pulling thistles.

10   Days on the Bog

Broken weather with heavy falls of rain and some strong winds set in during the third week of May. Mother seemed delighted.

"That's a grand drop o' rain," she enthused, "I'm a strong believer in the ould sayin' "A wet and windy May fills the haggard with corn and hay."

"Be the hevers o' war, it's very seldom wrong," said Grandad, "an' I'm sure ye often heard that other ould sayin', "A shower of rain in May is worth many loads o' hay."

The end of the week brought a return to fine weather again with few clouds in the sky and warm days that lasted to see out the month. Mike Casey, as he often did before, dropped in on us on Sunday and as usual, suggested a walk through the farm and over the bog. We gleefully gathered up the two dogs and accompanied him on the stroll with the customary good fun and banter along the way. It didn't take long to reach the bog road, then the little narrow path that led through the long ferns and on to that beautiful massive expanse of peatland, the Monettia bog.

"Begob, tomorrow's the fifth o' June an' I hope you lads know I'll be comin' early in the mornin' to start a bit o' dodgein', an' clane the bank for this year's turf," said Mike.

"Well, we wont be able to stay home from school tomorrow," I answered, "because the Inspector is comin' ."

"I wouldn't want any o' ye tomorrow or the next day, while I'm clanin' the bank," Mike replied, "but if ye want a lock o' fire in the grate this winter, I'd need a few wheelers on Friday and Saturday."

"We should be able to get Friday off alright,"

answered Christy, "but ye'd never be able to get all the turf cut it in two days."

"I know bloody well I wouldn't," said Mike, "but we'd do another two days next Friday and Saturday, an' finish it off at the end o' the month, when ye gang get yer school holidays."

Uncle Mike and his brother Tom arrived on Monday morning with spade and shovel strapped to the crossbar of their bicycles. After a quick "cup o' tay" from Mother they went direct to the bog. Dodgin' was the term used to describe the digging out of large cubes of light brown peat, known as dodges to a depth of three feet from the high bank of the virgin bog, to clear the new cutting area for the current year. The dodges were rolled down to fill in the previous year's bog holes and then levelled off. Bog holes, as they were called, were the water-filled craters left after last year's supply of turf had been cut away. The removal of these cubes of soft peat which of course was essential to expose the new cutting area, ideally served this purpose. Our midland bog varied from eleven to thirteen feet deep and the top three feet of poor consistency peat were light and spongy, and not at all suitable to convert to turf sods. So this low grade upper layer made an ideal filling for last year's excavations. Mike and Tom continued digging out the dodges and levelling off the bog holes until they had cleared a rectangular plot of approximately eight feet by eighteen feet. Then they evened off and smoothened the surface of this patch which they would later subdivide into three sections. Because Tom had come along to help Mike they completed the dodgin', cleaning and levelling by Tuesday evening and left the newly stripped sector to dry out until the turf cutting operation commenced at the end of the week.

Turf barrow. (Courtesy: Derryglad Folk Museum, Curraghboy, Athlone)

Friday morning the sun shone bright and early with scarcely a cloud in the sky. Mother advised we should wear a straw hat or some wide brimmed headgear in case of sunburn. Mike Casey arrived on his bicycle at nine o'clock. As customary he had his slane and light three-grained fork tied to the crossbar. The cutting blade of the slane and the prongs of the turf fork were sticking out backwards underneath his saddle.

"I tied them that way for safety," said Mike, with a broad grin on his face, "in case I ran into anybody."

As he took off his bicycle clips he told mother he already had his breakfast and didn't want anything to eat.

"O' course we wouldn't say no to a mugful o' tay around eleven," he continued, and then looking at us, "sure we wouldn't lads?"

"Oh, that's right," said Mother with a smile, "make sure ye give me plenty of exercise, whatever happens."

After donning some rare specimens of questionable headgear, Christy and Mick collected two turf barrows from the cart shed. We had one barrow of our own and borrowed the second one from Joe Fletcher who had already finished cutting for the current year. I filled a gallon of drinking water from the pump and Mother threw a handful of whole oatmeal into it saying, "That'll help to kill the thirst."

As we set off on the short trip to the bog, our youngest brother, Tim, came running up to Christy asking, "will ye give me a "jant" on the barrow?"

Christy agreed and no sooner had he loaded him up than Mother came bounding out to the first field shouting, "where d' ye think yer goin with him?

Turf cutting slane.

he's too young for the bog. D' ye want him to finish up in one of the bog drains?"

"I was only goin' to wheel him for a few yards," answered Christy.

"Well, wheel him for a few yards so," she replied in a blunt tone, "an' then bring him back to me."

When Christy lifted him off, after his brief jaunt, Tim started crying. However, the whinging was short lived when he got a firm promise he could travel to the bog when the eleven o' clock tay was being delivered to the turf-workers. Before we moved off, Mike, who carried the slane and turf fork, noticed that none of us had remembered to bring the spade.

"It's just as important as the fork," he shouted after Mick who raced back to the barn to collect it.

The surface of the new turf bank which Mike and Tom prepared on Monday and Tuesday now looked flat, dry and brittle with small patches, here and there where the crispy skin had actually cracked.

"Begob! that's great weather for cuttin' turf", said Mike, as he threw off his coat, rolled up his sleeves, spat on his hands and proceeded to mark out the initial cutting area with the spade. He then took the slane and I moved the barrow into position to load the first sods. They came fast and furious, faster than I could clear them.

"What the hell's houldin' ye up?" Mike enquired.

He kept his head bent downward with the broad brim of his straw hat obscuring any chance of getting a view of his face. However, I did manage to detect the end wrinkles of a grin on his jaw.

"Maybe you'd wheel, Mike, and I'll use the slane," I casually suggested.

"Ah! I'm only testin' ye out, Tommy an' actin' the Mick a bit, to keep ye on yer toes," he said as he burst out laughing.

"Well they nearly got yer name right when they called ye Mike," I replied, "they'd have done better if they had christened ye Mick."

Then with tears in his eyes from his hearty laugh and a look of satisfaction after his little joke, he settled down and delivered the heavy brown sods at a normal rate. I placed them on the barrow with the turf fork, two rows of five end to end across the barrow and one row down the centre, on top. The top row bound the bottom two together and helped to prevent the damp slippery sods from sliding off. The load was pretty heavy for a twelve year old. As I lifted the handles and moved off my bare feet sank and squelched in the soft peat, which the two men had used to fill and level the area the previous Monday during the dodgin' operations. While I struggled with my load away from the new bank, out across the narrow plank which bridged the main bog drain, Christy

Father Tom Prendergast, affectionately known as "Father Pinder".
(Courtesy: John Kearney, Offaly Historical and Archaeological Society, Tullamore)

moved in to fill his barrow. I knew I should be back again by the time he got loaded.

Out on the harder ground I managed to speed up a little, heeled over the barrowful of sods on to the dry turf-mouldy surface heavily punctuated with small tufts of heather, rushes and bog-cotton. Then I raced back, hauling the turf barrow behind and arriving just as Christy pulled out with his consignment. Uncle Mike, always known as a hard worker, kept up the pressure. Both of us scarcely had time to get over the bog drain, dump our load and get back before the other wheeler departed. After about an hour we introduced the third man, our special sub, Mick. When Christy or I tired or got out of breath we could alternately treat ourselves to a brief respite, while Mick moved in and took over our place for a few runs. Mick had just reached his ninth birthday so he couldn't fill the barrow as full as Christy and I. He only loaded one row of sods along each side and a half row down the middle. Nevertheless, his contribution proved significant.

The air remained calm and warm and the sun shone almost continuously with very few clouds in the sky to hinder it. From a vantage point on the high bank the waves of heather intermingling with tufts of white bog-cotton, blowing in the balmy June breeze, seemed to stretch in an unbroken sea all the way to Derrygunnigan wood on the east and well over the Laois border on the south. We were pleased indeed we had taken mother's advice regarding the straw hats and headgear to protect us from the first strong exposure of the year. Again, looking southwards across the heather laden high bank towards the little town of Clonaslee, we could see the heat waves dancing against the blue background of the Slieve Blooms, while high overhead the song of the skylark filled the air. Once or twice we heard the cuckoo. But now in the early days of June this joyous visitor, who had called loud and clear during the past weeks, seemed to be curtailing her appearances.

Almost on the dot of eleven o' clock Mother arrived with the usual "gallon" half full of tea and the well worn, brown, plastic shopping bag containing two slices of loaf bread and jam, each, for the four workers. True to her word she brought Tim with her and holding his hand, showed him the new turf bank and the barrowfuls of freshly cut sods as they lay drying in the sunshine. He relished his new found freedom especially being allowed perform long jumps on the soft springy surface while we took advantage of the very welcome break.

"I suppose ye're all goin' to the Sports on Sunday?" enquired Mike, as he watched young Tim endeavouring to gain a little extra distance each time he jumped.

"We certainly are," we all answered in chorus.

"Well, Father Prendergast has got them to do enough practicin' every evenin' for the past three weeks to win all the prizes in the country," answered Mother.

"Isn't Father "Pinder," as he is affectionately known,

"a wonderful man with the kids?" suggested Mike, "he'll be there on Sunday, as usual, with bags of oranges, apples and bananas for all the young ones."

"He passed us on his horse last Tuesday when we were comin' home from school," said Mick, "and told us to go back along the road a bit and see where the bird had laid eggs in the grass by the roadside. When we went back to where he directed us, we found a little pile of sweets, like Bulls eyes."

"Ah, sure he often did that with us too," added Christy.

"Well I hope this turf wheelin' doesn't lave ye too stiff for Sunday," said Mike.

Then emptying the dregs from his mug, and lighting a cigarette he suggested, "We better get back on the job before we're all sacked."

"There's a lot o' turf out there," said Mother, pointing to the newly cut crop, "an' I notice some of it is dark brown."

"Aye, we did well this mornin' ," answered Mike, it's bloody great turf. We hit the dark brown early this year."

"An' how many "boords" have ye cut?" queried Mother.

"We're about quarter way through the fifth floor," answered Mike, "an' I don't think we got the dark brown stuff last year until the sixth or seventh board.

"I wonder are we goin' to get a few extra floors o' black this year, so?" I asked.

"No, I think ye'll on'y get the usual two boords o' real black at the bottom," answered Mike, "but that manes yer goin' to get a few more boords o' top class dark brown."

"That's good news," said Mother, "sure the dark

brown is every bit as good as black for bakin' ."

Each layer or floor of sods taken off to a slane-head depth, might be known as a "Spit", a "Boord" (board), or a "Flure" (floor). By eleven o' clock Mike had cut four and a quarter floors. He would expect to see about six and a half cut and wheeled by dinner time, at one o' clock, and then the remaining three and a half to four difficult boards, taken out before quitting time at six o' clock in the evening. This could be considered a good day's work with three young wheelers, one of whom was little more than nine years of age. But many and varied were the stories of turf cutting feats as told in McEnroes public house at this time of the year. Young men in their early thirties and even older men in their fifties might boast of "finishin' two bog holes in one day, takin' eleven boords out of aich, with two wheelers". Of course the next yarn would out-do that one, "taking out twelve spit from two bog holes with two wheelers and then dodgin' enough to cover the next day's cuttin' ," and so on.

On resumption after dinner and when Mike had reached the seventh floor water began to seep in from last year's adjoining excavation. This appeared to be a standard occurrence each season and Mike dealt with the problem in the traditional way by leaving a narrow dam and capping it with "bog stuff", to prevent the water trickling in over the top. Leaving the dam unfortunately meant reducing the cutting sector, so the last four floors would lose almost two rows of sods. On reaching the seventh floor, the high bank now towered approximately nine feet above Mike's working area. In this situation it wasn't unusual, from time to time, for portions of the high bank to move or slip. So he had to take further precautions by cutting shallow steps into the low bank and one or two footholds in the dam to cover the possible eventuality of having to make a hasty exit. Luckily this time everything went well and no sooner had Mike cut the last few black sods from the tenth floor, and scrambled up his pre-arranged steps to the low bank, when the dam buckled and gave way under the pressure as water gushed in to cover the gravel at the bottom and then fill up to find a common level between the new and old bog holes.

"That could have been a close one," said Mike, as he wiped the bog-stuff from the handle of the slane. "I made a bags o' the dam, I should have tapered it to lave it stronger at the base."

"It doesn't matter now," said Christy, "it'll be well covered up by this time next year."

Just then, across the still air we could hear Mrs. Delaney ringing the Angelus bell in Killeigh church.

"That's six o' clock," said Mike, we've finished our first day on the bog an' we're still in one piece."

"God, look at you fellas," he continued, "yer feet and legs are in an awful state, ye better clane them up before ye head for home. Ye know the only way to get hardened bog stuff off yer skin is to use bog water."

While we scrubbed ourselves in the main bog drain which had a good depth of clear brown water, I became aware that my arms and knees were red and a little sore from sunburn.   Christy and Mick, for some reason, fared somewhat better. They were burned but not too sore, except for a small, irregular red patch on Christy's shoulder, where he had a tear in his shirt. It looked like a scrap of pink blotting paper and he cowered with the thought of anyone touching it.

Even at six thirty the sun rays were still warm. As we gathered up the tools and made our way homeward,

Uncle Mike remarked:-

"Ye know, I often think the bog draws the hate. One way or the other you fellas can forget about swimmin' in the glosh this evenin' . With burned arms an' legs like them ye'd never stand the soreness in the water an' ye wouldn't be able to dry yerselves when ye'd get out."

That sounded fair enough to us so we took his advice and stayed away from that popular resort on the Clodiagh river we called the glosh. Before going to bed that night, Mother, having first given us a dressing down for not protecting ourselves better against the sun, covered our sore patches with her special remedy made from unsalted butter and some other soothing ingredients only known to her.

Saturday dawned calm, dry and overcast with a warm haze blotting out the strong sun rays which had caused us so much trouble the previous day. It was an ideal morning for toasted skin to cool down and repair itself. Our legs and muscles showed no great ill effects from yesterday's labour and we turned in another creditable performance without showing any signs of stiffness. All the talk now centred on the Killeigh Sports on the morrow in Malones field. After the days work and a further application of that special sunburn cream, we went to an early bed fully confident of complete fitness for the following day.

Michael Malone and Father Prendergast had worked tirelessly to make this day a success. Killeigh Sports had a great reputation throughout Leinster and parts of Munster and attracted many well known athletes. Probably best known in former years for its famous cycle track on the village green. The Sports first took place in 1879 and the competing cyclists in these early years rode penny-farthing bicycles. One of the all-time greats who cycled in Killeigh before gaining fame in foreign parts was Alo Donegan, later to become the proud holder of two world titles.

While cycling races were still among the main events of the day, school-goers nevertheless got top priority, thanks to Father Prendergast. There were track races and other contests scheduled for children of all age groups and intending competitors could enter their names up to half an hour before the start. I entered the hundred yards sprint for twelve year olds, the high jump, long jump and the three-legged race with Christy as my partner, while he entered for the long jump and the sack race as well. Mick put his name down for the hundred yards sprint in the nine year old age group, the long jump and the egg and spoon race.

Father Prendergast, as Master of Ceremonies, kept a kindly eye on his favourite people - the school-goers. Sometimes marshalling his young competitors for the next event, arbitrating in the argument as to who came third in the under-sixes event or clearing us all off the track for the upcoming bicycle race. If at any time he suspected a youngster had used up all his sixpence or shilling pocket money on two-penny icecreams he came to the rescue with a big juicy orange or a shining red apple from what seemed to be a bottomless brown paper bag.

In the background, the "trick-o-the-loops", as Mother called them, were doing a roaring trade especially the man with the rings and coins. He used a small round table covered with a red tablecloth, on which he had arranged a selection of sixpence and shilling coins, with a half crown right in the centre. He charged threepence a go for five wooden rings with small centres, and the lucky punter who succeeded in throwing a ring clearly on to one of the coins, automatically won the coin netted. Of course, human nature

163

being what it is, most people tried unsuccessfully for the half crown, before they realised that the opening in the centre of the ring just barely fitted down over that coin. The Three-card-trick dealer did good business on his little square table with the three legs, as did the man who bent six inch wire nails with his bare hands. A piper and a melodeon player with their caps thrown on the grass, depended on the hospitality of the passers-by and a ticket seller offered a prize of a giant home made teddy bear.

Although delays plagued the starting time of almost every event, the organisers nevertheless succeeded in staging all the novelty items like egg and spoon race, sack race and so forth as well as the main contests. At the end of a great day when a good time was had by all, Christy and I felt proud when we stepped out to collect our prize as winners of the three-legged race and Christy had a further prize for coming second in the long jump. Later in the month we were delighted to read our names in the "Offaly Independent" of Saturday, the 17th June. When we arrived home and started to boast about our success, Mother chipped in,

"If it hadn't been for me curin' yer sunburn in time, ye wouldn't have won any prize at all."

In the days following, everybody still talked about the sports and how lucky we were with the weather. Christy, Mick and I were delighted that the turf wheeling stint didn't have any adverse affect on our leg muscles for the sprint races or the long jump. Of course secretly we were also thankful that the special sunburn cream worked wonders on our sore patches

After school each evening the following week we were given the job of hoeing potatoes, which were now well up over the ground. The hoeing operation was manual and meant clawing out the weeds from between each potato stalk as well as along the side of the drill and leaving them in the alley to die. A comparatively easy task, although somewhat monotonous. Mike Casey was coming to us again on Friday to continue the turf cutting and as grocery supplies were running low, Mother set out for the Tuesday market in Tullamore, bringing five dozen fresh hen eggs and six stone of hand picked Kerr's Pink potatoes. Although her wares did realise sufficient money to purchase bacon and other necessities for the turf workers, she sounded somewhat disappointed with the prices offered.

"Eight pence a dozen for eggs and seven pence a stone for potatoes, an' I'm told ten pence a pound for butter," she complained. "Sure last March I got a shilling a dozen for eggs and one and four pence a pound for butter."
She continued, "I bumped into Joe Condron an' he was tellin' me, he could only get twenty two shillings each for his ten week old sucks, and Tim Hickey had to sell his whiteheaded calf for fifty five shillings."

These prices did not really mean a lot to us but they did somehow register and if we heard other neighbours, at a later date, talking about butter at ten pence a pound or potatoes at seven pence a stone, we realised that in each case it was the buyer who got the bargain. However, having said that, we felt that no matter what price Mother got for her produce, she would still complain.

As arranged Mike Casey arrived early on Friday morning to continue with the turf cutting and by Saturday evening we had covered the complete area of dry bank on the outside of the main bog drain with barrowfuls of brown, dark brown and black turf. Every tuft of fern, heather and bog-cotton was now temporarily covered and would remain covered until the sods dried out sufficiently to foot. This area of turf represented three quarters of our requirements for the coming winter and spring. The remainder would be cut during the first week in July when the wheelers got their holidays.

Sunday the 18th of June, Mike called for me and we cycled in to Tullamore to see the Offaly minor hurling team play Kilkenny in the Leinster Championship and unfortunately the Offaly boys were routed. Kilkenny won on the score twelve goals and six points to two goals. One of the Kilkenny forwards, a lad by the name of T. O'Brien, scored six goals and two points of his County's total.

On Monday evening after school we watched Mother prepare to churn the large brown earthenware crock of cream

she had gathered over the past eight or nine days. She scrubbed out the tumble churn with boiling water, then rinsed it, poured in the cream, put the lid in position and screwed it down tightly with the four thumbscrews attached to the churn. After turning the handle for four or five minutes she suggested,

"Come on Tommy, ye might as well put yer hand to this for a few twists, while yer

Over-end churn. (Courtesy: National Museum of Ireland)

standin' there an' give yer mother a rest."

I eagerly took the handle and tumbled the churn faster than she had been going.

"Ah, hould on there, not so fast, ye'll destroy the butter," she rebuked. "Just a nice controlled motion, like I was doin'."

I steadied down to a slower pace and kept up the rotating action, until my right arm got tired.

"It's hard enough work," she said as she took the handle from me again and continued the operation herself.

"I think the butter is churned and ready," chirped Mick, more in mischief than in genuine concern.

With that, Mother stopped, pointed to the little glass window in the lid of the churn, and growled, "it's not ready until that glass is clear with a few small flecks of butter on it, can't ye see how blurred it is now? how many times have I to tell ye that?"

"Ah, sure I couldn't see the glass while the churn was spinnin' so fast," stammered Mick.

"Well now aren't ye very smart," quipped Mother, with a glint in her eye, "sure I thought anyone as smart as you, could see everything while the churn was in motion."

Mick, with a grin on his face and now realising he had got as good as he had given, shuffled a little further into the background. Just then, Paddy Poland arrived with a jug in his hand, looking for his daily ration of milk. Paddy had no cows of his own and collected a large jug of milk from us each day, sufficient to cover the needs of himself and his mother.

"Well begorrah Paddy, although I'm nearly finished, you better take a turn at this," said Mother, "or we'll have no butter."

The local belief was, that if anybody called while churning was in progress, he or she had to take a turn at the handle otherwise the butter would never form.

After alternating a few more stints at the handle the glass cleared and the butter was indeed ready. Using her two wooden butter spades, Mother carefully lifted out every last nodule of this golden bulky mass of new butter, placing it on a large blue plate, already lined with greaseproof paper or butter-paper as she preferred to call it. Later she would rinse it, add salt and embellish the top of each block with the decoration carved on the butter spade before wrapping in one pound lots. Prior to wrapping the final lot she measured out a certain portion, unsalted, to use for dressing run-of-the-mill cuts and wounds or as a base for her special sunburn cream. She then handed round a mugful of beautiful fresh buttermilk to all present.

When we got home from school on Tuesday evening and with normal chores completed, we had an extended

hurling practice in Kelly's field. On these long June evenings with darkness not descending until after half past ten, the hurling continued well beyond sunset. Kelly's farm adjoined ours so we didn't have far to walk. On our way home we heard through the calm warm air a sombre doleful sound, something like a distant foghorn. It appeared to be

Milk seperator. (Courtesy: Derryglad Folk Museum, Curraghboy, Athlone)

coming from the Cush or Gorteen direction and seemed to have two sources as if one was answering the other. Because we had experienced the phenomenon on other occasions we knew exactly what was happening. There were a couple of local lads hidden away in some hedge or copse, generating a wailing sound by blowing into the neck of a wine or spirit bottle. This practice survived more or less as a common custom in the parish, when an unfortunate man or woman, who happened to be unpopular with some small segment of the community had arranged his or her wedding date. The "Go boys," as Mother called them, blew bottles every evening, from some secluded place during the week or two weeks leading up to the wedding. I often wondered if this custom flourished in the traditions of any other part of Ireland.

At the end of the week I cycled down to Grannie's in Killeenmore to work with Tom Casey as he hoed the remaining drills of his potato crop. While there I became fascinated watching Mike in an adjoining field use an implement I had not seen before. He had borrowed it from his neighbour Frank Gowing and I found out it was called a Disc or Disc grub. In shape it resembled a turnip barrow but instead of having the hour-glass roller in front, it had two dish-like wheels. At the rear there were two twelve inch bright steel discs mounted at an angle to each other, in such a way, that the front edges were four or five inches apart, while the back edges were more than double that distance from each other. Mike was using the implement on beet drills in the moor which had sprouted more than their fair share of weeds. The discs had the effect of peeling off the shoulder of weeds on each side, and thereby reducing the width of the drill to approximately four inches leaving it much easier for thinning.

"It's a bloody great yoke," said Mike. "I'm surprised ye hadn't seen it before now, with some of the Ballinvalley gang. I've a couple o' fellas lined up to start thinnin' here in a day or two, an' I'll bet the disc'll have half the job done for them."

"An' sure the dry warm weather will help the weeds to die quickly as well," I added.

Mike continued, "The comin' Sunday I think is the twenty fifth o' June, an' we'll be cuttin' the remainder of our own hay during the first few days of next week."

"That'll be our last week in school," I enthused. "We'll be gettin' our holidays on Friday, the thirtieth."

"Well, I'll probably start cuttin' your lock o' scutch on the Friday, and maybe finish the lot on Saturday."

"Seein' it's our last day, I might make an effort to stay home and maybe do something for ye," I suggested.

"Well, begob if ye do, I wont be the one to object," said Mike with a grin.

Discing turnip drills at Fenter, Killeigh, 1930's. (Courtesy: John Kearney, Offaly Historical and Archaeological Society, Tullamore)

Drill disk grub.

When we told Grandad the news, he wasted no time in oiling every moving part of our Adriance Buckeye mowing machine. He then spent two days sharpening each triangular section on the two machine knives which were kept from year to year on the rafters in the barn, rolled up in greasy sacking to prevent rust. Although in his middle seventies he was very handy with the sharpening stone or carborundum as he preferred to call it. The machine knives had sixteen sections with two cutting edges on each section. He honed all the blades to perfect sharpness and then replaced the two knives in their greasy cover. On Friday morning Christy and I got up earlier than usual and had the two horses tackled and ready by the time Mike arrived. As it worked out neither of us could get permission to stay home from school so Mike had to carry on on his own. That didn't pose much of a problem because cutting hay is really a one man job. He seemed pleased enough to find two bright, well sharpened knives ready for use.

"I remember, this time last year I had to sharpen the bloody things myself before I could make a start," he said with a look of surprise.

He then proceeded to slip one of the knives through the fingers of the finger-beam and coupled it to the wooden

The author's brother, Christy, preparing to cut hay at Uncle Mike Casey's farm, Killeenmore, in the late 1940's. (Courtesy: John Kearney, Offaly Historical and Archaeological Society, Tullamore)

connecting rod.

"I often wondered why Adriance Buckeye used a wooden connecting rod while Samuelson always favoured a metal one," he mused.

I'm sure this question crossed Mike's mind because his own mowing machine was in fact a Samuelson. He fitted the grass board in position, threw a half filled sack of straw on to the metal seat as a cushion, moved the finger-beam up to its safety angle and drove his team across the short trip to the "field forninst the door."

It was a pleasant morning with a mild southerly breeze blowing in from the bog and enough breaks in the cloud cover to persuade Mike to wear his wide brimmed straw hat. By the time we arrived home from school he had cut four acres of this five acre field. In the distance we could hear the rich, metallic whine from the gears and gear housing, so distinctive of the Adriance Buckeye and as we neared the meadow where Mike was working, a tantalising fragrance of new mown hay filled the air. A flock of cheeky crows strutted through the freshly cut swards while a thrush

The Corncrake.

piped out some non-stop symphony from the topmost branch of the oak tree at Purcell's corner.

"What the hell do the crows be lookin' for in hay, Mike?" asked Christy.

"Well," Mike answered, "they'd get plenty of insects, moths, slugs an' things like that an' then a lot o' frogs get cut up, or lose legs an' arms with the machine an' the ould crows make short work o' the fragments."

Mike wiped the perspiration from underneath the sweatband of his straw hat and the firm, bony features of his suntanned face broke into a broad grin as he spotted the tattered brown shopping bag in Christy's hand, which told him we had brought "a drop o' four o' clock tay." He halted his team on the headland, ensuring that the horses were in the shade of the tall ivy-covered hawthorns. Mick gave them a handful of the newly mown hay, and noticed they were steaming hot underneath the druman and collar.

"Ah, don't worry Mick, it's natural for horses to sweat on a day like that," said Mike, "sure we're all sweatin', they'll soon cool down there in the shade."

Mike made short work of the mugful of tea and the two slices of bread and marmalade.

"Sure I'll have no bother finishin' off the remainder o' that hay in an hour or so," he said, lighting a cigarette, and looking at the remaining square of standing meadow. "A corncrake ran out there about ten minutes ago an' disappeared through the briars in the far ditch," he told us, pointing towards the hedge on the opposite side of the field.

"I think there may be another one in there still," he continued, "so maybe you fellas might hunt her out before I start up the machine agin."

No sooner said than done, the three of us ran helter skelter into the long meadow grass, making all sorts of weird sounds and clapping our hands as we ran. Sure enough two more nervous corncrakes emerged and sped to the safety of the undergrowth in the hedgerow.

"Well done lads," shouted Mike as he took the reins and sat back up on the mowing machine, "I'd hate to see the legs being cut off the poor divils."

He finished cutting the remainder of the meadow before tea time, leaving only four acres to be cut in the ould house field on Saturday. Lying in bed that night we could hear two or three corncrakes crake-craking their rasping call from the direction of the ould house field and we knew then that the three, which had taken refuge in the hedgerows of the field Mike had just cut, were now probably sheltering in the more secure cover of the only remaining meadow. The ould house from which this field got it's name could only be described now as a nettle covered ruin. In earlier days it was the childhood home of our great grandmother, Mary Catherine Byrne.

Of course there was no school on Saturday the first of July so once again we had the horses tackled and ready for Mike when he arrived. Because we knew he was concerned, we told him about hearing the corncrakes the previous night.

"Well, there's no danger for a good while at the beginnin' ," said Mike. "They'll keep runnin' all the time towards the centre so when I'm about half way through the job, sometime after dinner, you lads can gallop in an' hunt them out agin. The big problem o' course is if they're

Hay tumbling rake.

nestin', the horses' feet or the wheels o' the machine will break up the eggs."

The plan worked fairly well and on this occasion we actually hooshed out and saved the lives of four birds. Unfortunately, when all the hay was cut we found one nest with four badly crushed eggs. However, Uncle Mike suggested, because there were four corncrakes there was probably a second nest in a safe area in the undergrowth near one of the hedges. He also told us that the corncrake which lost its nest would build a new one and start all over again.

Helping at the hay. Some of the Author's children with their cousins at Mick's (Author's brother) Haggard, Cloncollog, Tullamore. 1969.

11   Saving the Hay

We are now into the first week of July, the start of our school holidays, but for us that really means we enter a period of full-time work on the farm, until we return to school in the early days of September. As fate would have it, July and August could certainly be described as the two busiest months of the year on the land. Our first few days were spent at the backbreaking chore of "spreadin' an' turnin' turf." The turf which we wheeled two and three weeks earlier was thrown down in barrowfuls on to the short heather, sedge-grass and rushes.   By now the surfaces exposed to the sun and wind had dried out considerably, but surfaces covered by other sods and the under side of sods lying flat against the bog were still very damp.   We had to spread out and scatter the piles more thinly and turn the wet side of every sod upwards to dry. Later in the week and with the same three wheelers as before, Tom Casey finalised the remainder of our turf cutting for the season.

That done, Christy, Mick and I turned our hands to thinning beet and mangolds while Tom Casey took charge of the red mare, to gather the hay into windrows on the two cut meadows using the tumbling rake. After two days thinning, with pollard sacks tied around our knees, wrists paining with "tawlock" and hands stained green from pulling spunk, chickenweed and dandelions, more commonly known as sow-thistles, we were indeed pleased to learn our assistance was needed elsewhere. We were co-opted to tram hay with Tom Casey and Paddy Poland. Even mother and Tim gave a hand as well. Tom, still with the red mare and tumbling rake, hauled in the supplies of hay to the tram makers who

Field of Haycocks. (Courtesy: Derryglad Folk Museum)

followed a pre-arranged plan. Mother and Christy brought the tram or cock up to a little more than half way, then Paddy Poland and I put in the final touches and headed it off while Christy and Mother went on to start a new one. Tim, using a short handled rake, gathered up all the loose traineens around the cock as Paddy and I moved away.

The outdoor production team worked exceptionally well while Mary and Margaret co-ordinated all activities in the kitchen and ably looked after teabreaks and dinners. After toiling full out for four beautiful sunny days, including Sunday we had, between the two fields, put up sixty two cocks of first grade hay. The trams would now be left to settle for seven or eight days, and Grandad insisted,

"They should get a final headin' off, like they always did in my young days."

Headin' off consisted of "pullin' the butts", in other words, pulling out the loose skirt of hay right around at ground level, settling it neatly on top of the cock and then tying down the whole lot with two hay ropes. Using a roughly constructed twister made of strong wire, the hay ropes were expertly woven from the bottom of the cock in one piece and fastened tightly, deep into the hay, low down on the other side. One rope running north south across the top and the other running east west. They were exceptionally strong and helped in no small way to save damage to the hay cocks in wet and windy conditions.

With the hay saved we had to return to probably the most unpopular job of all, completing the thinning of beet and mangolds. Thankfully, for the remainder of this task Mother organised the help of two of our local school pals who were delighted to earn one and sixpence a day for their labours. The July weather continued warm and sunny, brilliant evenings for swimming in the Glosh, the sun beaming down almost continuously for days and days. Unfortunately, from the thinning point of view this also constituted a down side. It left the soil hard, dry and abrasive, tearing little flecks of skin from around our fingernails from the constant thrusting and grasping which is part and parcel of the thinning process. It left portion of our shins and thighs scalded with the heat from the pollard sacks we had tied on like spats to protect our knees. Were we happy to see the thinning finished? You could hear the yippees in Killurin when the last little pale yellow mangold plant stood naked and alone at the end of the final drill.

It is now Saturday the fifteenth of July, Saint Swithin's Day, and no sign of a break in the weather. Grandad, reading the "Offaly Independent", suddenly remembers the date, leaves down his paper and proceeds to quote his seasonal quote:-

Saint Swithin's Day if it dost rain,
Forty days it will remain.
Saint Swithin's Day if it be fair,
Forty days 'twill rain nae maer.

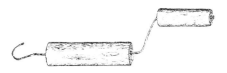

Twister used for making hay ropes.
(Courtesy: Department of Irish Folklore U.C.D.)

"Well, be the hevers o' war it looks as if we're goin' to have another forty days o' fine weather if Saint Swithin is right," he continued.

"Sure there's nothin' wrong with that, Grandad," ventured Christy.

"Well, I know we've our own hay cut and saved, a' tan a rate," he replied, "but there's a lot o' people who haven't even got it cut yit, an' they're worried they'll have a very poor return, with all this dry weather."

With that he returned to his reading, and advised us that the Twelfth o' July celebrations in Belfast had passed off quietly. "The speeches lacked the usual fire and vigour," he said.

Monday we headed off to the bog again, this time to foot the turf. The sods had by now dried out reasonably well on all sides but to help the process further, it was necessary to put them into "footins." First of all, four sods were propped against each other on end in an east west, north south formation. Two were laid horizontally across the top of these then one more over that at right angles to the first two and topped off with a broken or half clod.

To make the job less monotonous and a little more interesting we measured off little square areas and then set ourselves time limits to finish each square; say, by eleven o' clock tay, dinner time, four o' clock tay or before quitting time. It might be the case that we set ourselves the task of doing two of these allotments within some of the time limits. The psychology worked because it saved us from visualising the awesome vista, of the vast area as a whole. We therefore concentrated on the much smaller plot we mapped out for ourselves and the task never felt quite so daunting.

Most evenings after our hard day's toil we made our way to the Glosh, dipping, splashing and paddling being the order of the day in the cool mountain water of the Clodiagh. None of us had really mastered the art of swimming and this presumably accounted for one of the reasons we were not allowed to visit the new swimming pool in Tullamore. One of the first civic swimming pools to be opened in Ireland. Mr. Sean T. O'Kelly, Minister for Local Government, had performed the opening ceremony in May of the previous year. It proved to be a catch twenty two situation for us. Our mother wouldn't allow us to visit it because we were not able to swim and of course we had little chance of learning unless we were allowed to go there for lessons. However, that never really bothered us too much while we continued to have our share of good wholesome fun at the Glosh.

All around us now almost every neighbour worked on some phase of hay saving. Fantin Kerwin like us had all his crop cut and trammed and was now busy, with his daughter Bridgie, headin' off the cocks. Freddie Colton, with a large acreage under hay, had fields at many different stages. Some were trammed others in grass-cocks while some additional meadows had still to be cut. Freddie didn't like the idea of windrows during this dry year and made grass-cocks instead before tramming.

"The hay is too dry as it is, without lettin' it dry any further in windrows," Freddie told us. "It holds it's moisture better, in grass-cocks."

Apparently Jim Connolly had different ideas. He had the bulk of his crop saved and trammed as we enviously looked at him sitting high up on a gig-rake, smoking his pipe while gathering windrows in the last of his meadows.

"I'd love a job like that," said Mick, "sittin' up on a comfortable seat, just pullin' a lever now and again and gatherin' the hay far faster than you did walkin' after that ould tumblin' rake," he said, addressing Christy.

"I suppose it's all a question o' money," replied Christy, "we'd have one too if we could afford it."

Then came the best news of all, we heard Con Kelly had plans to start drawing in hay on Monday. Of course that meant his brother, Charlie, would be operating the hay-lifter and this certainly represented a phase in the hay saving season which fascinated us young fellas. To make things better, we heard he intended starting in Osborne's field beside Poland's lane which was no more than three hundred yards from our dwelling house. As far as we were concerned, drawing in hay could in many ways be compared to a mini thrashin' because it involved a reasonably large and intricate piece of machinery and at the same time was labour intensive.

Hay gig rake. (Courtesy: Wexford County Library)

We were up and out early on the Monday, having previously obtained permission from our mother to "take the mornin' off."

"Ah, ye've worked hard at the hay an' the bog," she agreed. "Ye can take a few hours to watch the lifter but don't go too near it."

The warning drifted over our heads because we intended getting a close-up view of the works. Charlie Kelly was a genial man and we knew he would be careful enough to keep an eye out for any impending danger. There were two men back in Kellys' haggard to make the rick, two more to pitch the hay when the cocks started arriving, two with horses and carts drawing in the hay from the field to the haggard and then Charlie operating the horse-drawn lifter in the hay field.

The lifter looked like the uncovered framework of a giant metal tepee, mounted on two wheels. Three chains, to which long steel lifting arms were attached at an angle of eighty degrees dangled from a nest of complicated, robust pulleys at the apex. Charlie manoeuvred the lifter into place so as to position the haycock in the centre of the three upright stanchions. The chains were lowered down to ground level and the three lifting arms pushed right in underneath the cock, equidistant from each other. With the lifting arms firmly in place, Charlie operated a winding handle attached to a combination of well oiled gears which wound up the chains and raised the haycock high enough above the ground, to allow the horse cart to be backed in underneath. With the cart in position, he reversed the winding operation and gently lowered the haycock on to the cart. The driver then drove his horse and load of hay back to the haggard and Charlie moved on to the next cock to load the second driver.

We thought it marvellous seeing the heavy haycocks being lifted high into the air and couldn't understand how Charlie could lift all this weight by merely turning a handle.

"Ah, it's too complicated for you fellas to grasp, it's all a question of gear ratio," he said.

It took us weeks to find out what he was talking about and one day when we told him we had a fair idea of what he meant by gear ratio, Charlie said with a grin,

"Well if ye have, ye'll have to explain it to me another time, because I don't understand it either."

We continued to follow him around the field, staring in undiminished amazement at each tram being hoisted up and loaded. Some small field mice ran out from underneath several cocks. On two occasions we found little pink clutches of their young lying curled up with eyes closed in the musty hay stubble where the tram rested. We assumed and hoped the mother would return as soon as the haymakers moved on.

Metal haylifter. (Courtesy: National Museum of Ireland)

By dinner time, the new rick, back in Kellys' haggard had reached a height of five or six feet and the incoming loads were arriving faster than the two pitchers could toss them on to the rick makers. However, after dinner when all the cocks were cleared from the field, one of the drivers returned with his horse and cart and collected the loose remnants of scattered hay, which the lifter arms failed to grab or which fell off while the cocks were being hoisted. That done he helped the two pitchers to catch up on their backlog, thus leaving only one man drawing in. Meantime Charlie Kelly tied up all loose ends on the lifter, lit his pipe and prepared to move on to the next theatre of operation just about half a mile away. Our tummies now told us we had done enough viewing and gallavanting for the morning so with a hop and a skip we headed back home, told Mother about our experiences and then made short work of some overdue dinners.

We are now well into the third week of July. The corn crops, - wheat, oats, and barley and the root crops, - beet, turnips and mangolds are doing as well as could be expected in the dry spell.

"A few good showers o' rain would do no harm at all," suggested Grandad, as he looked out across the first field.

"Awe, give us a chance, Grandad," we said in unison, "we don't want any rain until we get the turf heaped."

"The divil a harm a drop o' rain would do it, now that it has a good hard dry skin," he replied.

Heaping turf did not demand the same delicate approach as did footing, we could take the sods in handfuls rather than handling each turf individually. Before we commenced, mother warned us -

"It's so dry, be sure ye make good big hapes," and this we did.

First we threw the footings into large rough piles at regular intervals. Then with what looked to us like the craft of a seasoned clamp maker, we built up a regular wall of sods on the outside of the heap and kept filling the centre with broken fragments as well as with whole pieces.

We proceeded like this with each heap while all the time moulding the structure slowly into an orderly cone-like shape. The black turf proved hard to handle. The surface on the sods had baked and cracked open with the heat of the sun, leaving sharp pointed edges which irritated little flecks of skin, around the nails of our fingers, just as the hard soil did when we were thinning the beet. Nevertheless it turned out to be a job our youngest brother, Tim, enjoyed. He felt so important collecting and handing up brown sods of uniform shape, which we used in the construction of the outer walls of the heaps. Each finished pile had the nap of the outside layer of sods, arranged in such a way so as to ensure that rain spilled off the surface rather than soak into the turf. After work each evening while on this assignment, we treated our sore fingers with Vaseline or a small application of our special sunburn cream. Much to all our delight we finalised the heaping in three days. Now we knew for the next instalment, - the drawing home of the turf, - we could use beet forks to load it instead of hurting our hands.

12   Cutting the Corn

The calendar moved forward to the last week of July and this brought a break in the weather with heavy rain and some strong winds. Mother wasn't too perturbed.

"All the crops could do with a drop o' that rain," she suggested, "the ground is far too dry."

"It's welcome enough now," agreed Grandad, "but I hope it's not the beginnin' of a wet harvest."

We too, were pleased to see it raining because on wet days very little work could be done and as we had been going hammer and thongs now for almost four weeks, we greeted the raindrops with some enthusiasm. The broken weather saw July out and continued into the first week of August. Luckily, it caused no great damage to grain crops. There were no serious reports from any district of wheat or barley being lodged.

"I always think the rain, as well as the sun, helps to ripen the barley," said Grandad, almost apologising for the wet conditions.

"Well, I never heard that before," answered Mother, "an' I think we have had enough rain now. I hope it gets back to those warm dry days soon agin."

During the off days Uncle Mike used up his time cleaning, repairing and oiling the Massey Harris reaper-and-binder in readiness for the coming harvest season. Some of our neighbours were taking advantage of whatever fine hours were available, to heap and wheel out turf to the loading point, for drawing home. The cleeve or kish - a large, shallow, oval or rectangular basket-like container, made from sally wattles or young hazel saplings, mounted on an ordinary turf barrow was used for wheeling out. Pat Sheeran, as usual kept ahead of everybody. He had all his turf ready for collection and now devoted his days to drawing it home. Pat's only mode of conveyance lay in his sturdy donkey and cart. He faced a three mile trek from dwelling house to turf bank so no surprise then, that he always fitted a nice set of blue wooden creels to the cart, enabling him to bring a worthwhile load. In the coming days most folks would make a genuine effort to get their own turf supply carted home and clamped before the harvest proper got under way.

Making a good clamp to withstand the rigours of winter rains was, like the potato pit in October, a special art. The best and most uniform sods were used in the construction of the outside wall or shell and the angle of the base of the sod, in relation to the side, expertly utilised to virtually draw the clamp to a point at the apex. In assembling this outside wall of the clamp, I had seen Mike Casey, Fantin Kerwin or Grandad, on occasions, testing and weighing up in their hands, five or six different sods before deciding they had chosen the one with the correct angle or lie. The top of the clamp was always covered over with shovelfuls of turf mould and then squares of old canvas or sacking thrown over the top and tied down with weights.

The cuckoos are now silent and preparing for their long migration flight back to North Africa. Their young ones, reared by willow warbler, robin or meadow pipit search for grubs, caterpillars and other food morsels, unaware that the large greyish bird they are competing with could in fact be their real father or mother. The dawn chorus which we came to know and love so well during the spring and early summer is now sadly, almost no more. In the hedgerows there is an abundance of blackberries, helped on to the ripening process by the mid-August sun and in the "Ould garden" the young apples are maturing nicely.

It seemed most unusual for Joe Fletcher to be late in drawing in his hay but this year, for some reason, he certainly was. Joe never favoured the hay-lifter for this operation and always preferred the hay bogey. He considered the lifter to be "slow, ponderous and a waste of good pitching time." As he drove past our house with the first hay cock from the Red hill, I pleaded with Mother to let me travel with him for a few journeys. Journey was the correct term because Joe's land holding in the Red hill was surely three miles away from his main acreage. He affectionately referred to this section of his land as "Donegal," being so far distant from the principal farm.

Getting jants on a hay bogey represented one of our special summer treats and delights. When Christy and Mick heard the news, they too, quickly organised their travel permit. These jants, three miles out and three miles back, were really worth while and as Joe had no family of his own, was quite happy to have, as he said himself, "a few hardy young fellas with me." The hay bogey, this low-loader with its glossy wooden floor polished smooth from the fine

Hay bogey. (Courtesy: Wexford County Library)

Sharpening the scythe.
(Courtesy: Department of Irish Folklore,
University College Dublin)

abrasive action of hay cocks slipping up or down along it's surface, seemed almost as broad as it was long. It had plenty of space to accommodate a gaggle of youngsters and not too far to fall if we slipped, or more likely were pushed off the back end on to the meadow. Indeed this formed the main part of the fun, pushing each other off into the deep soft sward of new after-grass. The lush green growth which sprang up after meadows were cut and saved was known as after-grass. It often provided much needed grazing for cows and cattle in dry summers when their usual feeding grounds were already stripped bare.

Each time Joe arrived at the hay field in the Red hill, Con Poland, who lived close by, came across to winch up the haycock with him. The bogey was horse drawn and had two shafts like an ordinary cart. By operating a lever underneath, it heeled up on it's back edge and could then be reversed in under the base of the haycock. Two extra strong bogey ropes, which were attached to either extremity of a ratchet roller at the front of the bogey, were extended and hooked together down low at the back of the cock. By operating in pump like fashion, two handles which activated the ratchet roller, the haycock could be slowly hauled up along the floor of the bogey. When it passed the half-way point, the weight of the hay caused the bogey to level off then the locking mechanism underneath snapped closed. The load was now ready for the homeward trip with plenty of space still available to accommodate Joe's young passengers.

We only succeeded in getting the one day off travelling with Joe. Unfortunately, we had to do a stint in Killeenmore helping uncle Mike to heap the remainder of his turf. I say unfortunately because this meant we were again going to finish up with sore fingers. At the end of four days Joe had drawn in all his hay both from Donegal and his local farm. This represented forty four cocks standing side by side in his haggard and as we passed we could only surmise and wish if we had them in our own haggard we might stay out all night playing hide-and-seek.

It's now a little past mid-August and first reports of corn cutting in the Daingean area were the chief topics of discussion after second Mass among the men who each Sunday and Holy day congregated just across the road from the church gates in Killeigh. Mike and Tom Casey usually took up position in this group to smoke their cigarettes and keep up to date with local gossip. As I was at late Mass I slipped over to talk with Mike and attempted to inveigle him up to our house in the afternoon for a walk and a yarn and maybe a game of cards later. While there, I overheard the information that quite a few acres of wheat and oats had been cut around Daingean and Geashill, that the grain turned out to be bone dry and the yield looked very promising.

On Monday the fourteenth of August it caused no surprise to me when I heard that familiar and nostalgic sound of a sharpening stone resounding off the hard steel blade of a scythe. Grandad was the culprit, busily honing it in preparation to open out the headlands of the oats crop in the Turn field. Taking out the first sward with a scythe, right around the four boundaries of the corn field to leave walking space for the horses when the reaper-and-binder came along to cut the crop proper, was known as "opening out the headlands."

Nobody could sharpen or use a scythe better than Grandad, at least that's what he figured. We watched in silence as he stood with the double curved handle resting behind him on the barn floor. His left hand holding the long blade steady over his left shoulder, while he swished the sharpening stone in short staccato movements, up one side then down the other, all the while ensuring the stone maintained a special angle against the blade. Then he added a flurry of circular movements as if to finalise the honing at that particular point.

To me, this scythe sharpening sound, like the cuckoo in springtime or the corncrake in June always conjured up a wistful feeling of nostalgia. Obviously not on my own in this regard, I read some sentimental words by the late Monica Carr in her most engaging "Country Diary," on the same subject.

"We still have a scythe hanging in the shed," says Monica, "and I often find myself stroking it, as I pass. Summer days of yesteryear there was always the swish of grass falling under the scythe blade, the keenness of which was achieved with a sharpening stone. And all the while there would be talk. Tales told by my father, of what it was like in his young days, when 'men were men,' and the ambition was to 'shave the fur off the back of a sleeping mouse' without waking it up."

When he had the blade honed to his satisfaction,

Massey-Harris, reaper and binder. (Courtesy: Irish Agricultural Museum, Johnstown Castle, Wexford)

Grandad made his way to the Turn field carrying the scythe in one hand and a sharpening stone in the other. He needed a helper so he collared me to follow him, gather the oaten stalks and tie them into sheaves as he cut the sward ahead of me. Although in his mid-seventies, his mowing movement was rhythmical. With bowed shoulders and feet apart he held the two short grips in either hand and swished the shining blade from right to left, each time taking a neat four-inch bite into the golden corn. I gazed at him enthralled as he made stroke by stroke, all the time shuffling his feet forward to be in position for the next sweep. He had fitted an ingenious guide-wire to the scythe, in the form of a sally wattle looped upright from the handle to the heel of the cutting blade. As he swept each cutting stroke through the oats the guide helped to gather the stalks into one neat ridge, on the left hand side of the sward. When he had gone ten or twelve yards, he stopped for a break and I moved in to gather the cut corn into sheaves.

"I hope ye haven't forgotten how to make a double band? he questioned, as he wiped the sweat from his forehead.

"Ah, sure I could give ye lessons on how to do that, Grandad," I answered, as I knocked the first sheaf into shape. Then, to let him see I wasn't bluffing, I took a small fistful of strands from the sheaf, held it in both hands with palms facing upwards and quickly twisted the heads in a loop, back underneath the straws, at the same time dividing the butt ends into two equal portions. Then I put the new elongated binding around the sheaf, twisted the two butt ends around each other and pushed the resultant fly ends securely underneath the band.

"Well, be the hevers o' war, I couldn't make a double band any quicker or any better than that, meself," said Grandad, as he prepared to resume work with the scythe.

"It's a thrifty way to do the job," he continued, "because at thrashin' time, whin the band is cut it can go into the drum the same time as the shafe itself so no grain is lost."

Mike Casey cutting wheat with reaper and binder. August 1940. Tom Murray (Author) is at the rear)

The oat crop was healthy and clean with scarcely a tall weed, no thistles, poppies or seedy docks. Nevertheless, in gathering in the sheaves I handled each armful gingerly.

My memories of opening out the headlands, of the previous year's barley crop with Mick in the moor field, where we had forgotten to use the thistle-puller in the spring, were still vivid. Along one headland there were thistles in almost every handful. We had to stop regularly to remove thorns from each other's fingers and finished the day with arms chafed, red and sore. With Grandad taking so many rests and time out to sharpen the scythe, it took almost a day and a half to open the four headlands. During our second day, Mother went to Tullamore with Kerry, the red pony to get amongst other things, eight bales of binder twine for the harvest operations coming up.

Mike Casey arrived in the Turn field on Thursday morning with the Massey Harris reaper-and-binder. The August sun shone in an almost cloudless sky, with heat ripples clearly visible dancing above that vast sweep of golden gorse and purple heather, which was graphically outlined against the dark blue of the mountains to the south. Only a narrow area of furze bushes separated the Turn field from this area of cut-away bog. The broad expanse of the uncut virgin bog which stretched away in the distance to the foothills of the Slieve Blooms proudly displayed its massive blanket of purple heather, broken only here and there by the white unkempt hair-dos of some small patches of bog cotton. A slight breeze meandered in from the east, scarcely strong enough to flutter an aspen leaf. The few small clouds in view looked more like tiny curved feathers floating in the dome of the sky.

"Them goat beards or mare's tails were always a sign

o' good weather," said Grandad, nodding his head skywards, as if trying to point out the tiny wisps of cloud.

"Yer right, Boss," said Mike, "an' that little breeze from the east'll keep us from burnin' up altogether durin' the hate o' the day." Then in a humourous tone added, "why the hell don't ye get rid o' that crooked fairy tree, in the middle o' the field?"

"You ask that same question, Mike, every year there's corn in this field," answered Christy, out of earshot of Grandad, "an' ye know well that Ould Geg (grandad) wont let anyone touch it never mind gettin' rid of it."

"Well, Ould Geg might change his mind, if he had to manoeuvre a team o' horses and a reaper-and-binder around it, a few times," challenged Mike.
Just then Tom Casey arrived.

"What the blazes is goin' on here?" queried Tom, "wastin' good harvest weather arguin' over a bloody hawthorn bush, an' not a blade o' corn cut."

With a loud guffaw uncle Mike walked around to the rear of the reaper-and-binder collected his tool box, lowered the main ground wheel and took off the two road wheels. While he was so engaged, Mick and I hooked up the team of horses and put a ball of twine into the twine box. Mike then threaded the twine through a series of eyes and arms, finishing up at the little complex steel fingers which actually knotted the twine around each sheaf, before the kicker arms consigned it to the ground below. As a final inspection he checked if the canvas table, which acts as part of a conveyor system when the machine is in motion, remained taut, and then adjusted the height of the cutting blade. With everything now ready he took the reins, stepped on to the running board at the rear of the canvas table and hoisted himself on to the driving seat. He coaxed the horses into position, slipped the binder into gear and with his usual pre-work exclamation, "In the name o' God," moved off his team of three and set the big machine in motion.

The first day of harvest, it was indeed a thrill and an awe inspiring moment for us seeing the bulky apparatus spring to life. The revolving wooden arms or reels as they were called, so tall against the skyline, pressing the grain stalks against the cutting blades. The whirring drone of the knife. The newly cut strands of golden corn falling on to the moving canvas and being wafted frantically up the conveyor system to be compacted into the first sheaf. We walked around following the binder for two or three circuits of the field, still in wonder of the hidden mechanical man who tied sheaf after sheaf before methodically tossing them to the ground in a uniform line. Suddenly our dream world was drastically upset.

"What the hell are you fellas up to?" shouted Tom Casey. "Are ye goin' to walk around after that yoke all day, scratchin' yerselves? There's three rows o' shaves here to be stooked as well as the hand-tied row along the ditch."

The three of us, Christy, Mick and I recognised the urgent note in Tom's voice, and quickly scampered across to where he had already made up three or four stooks.

"Come on lads, ye'll have to get movin'; he's throwin' out shaves there at an awful rate," said Tom, motioning towards the binder.

There and then we set up two crews, Christy and I worked together, Mick teamed up with Tom and we all took turns collecting the hand-tied sheaves along the ditch. These, of course, were from the sward cut earlier by grandad when opening out the headlands. Being an oat crop, which is comparatively light, the stooks consisted of six sheaves standing in a three against three formation. Alternatively, if stooking barley we would probably use four sheaves only, lying against each other in an east west, north south formation. Then in the case of wheat, we would of course make cap-stooks. The oat stooks we were now making would be left standing for five or six days before putting them into stacks. This further assisted the ripening process and facilitated the withering of weeds and grass in the butt of each sheaf.

After the binder had completed a few more circuits Grandad arrived out on the headland carrying the scythe and a wooden rake. He was certainly dressed for the weather, wearing a battered, brown straw hat that surely had seen better days and an open waistcoat over his blue striped shirt. The shirt sleeves were rolled up almost to his shoulders.

"What the blazes did he bring those yokes with him for?," said Christy, more or less as an aside, when he saw what Grandad was carrying.

"Well, more power to yer elbow," shouted Mike, as he approached the nearby corner and brought the horses to a halt, before turning in on the next bout.

"I hope yer goin' to give me a bit o' clearance around that bloody ould fairy tree."

"Be the hevers o' war, Mike, that's exactly why I brought the scythe with me," smiled Grandad, "but be careful what ye say about that fairy bush."

"Hard luck, Tommy," said Christy to me, under his breath, "yer goin' to get a call any minute now to take out the shaves around the fairy tree, when "Geg" starts cuttin' ."

No sooner had he said it, than I got the call. As I moved off to follow Grandad, Tom Casey added his taunting remark.

"Ye'll want to watch yer fingers over there, Tommy; there's a lot o' ould briars and nettles around the butt o' the tree."

Well fate was kind enough, we cut and bound two wide swards encircling the area of the tree without encountering any nettles or thorns.

"That's a grate job, fellas, it'll make it much asier to get this contraption around it now," shouted Mike, as he passed by on the next circuit.

Before mid-afternoon the last remaining stalks of oats were committed to sheaves and within the hour the two field crews had assembled the final stook. We then gave a hand to Mike to fit road wheels and generally re-equip the reaper-and-binder for it's trip back to Killeenmore. Mike intended cutting his own corn crops during the following week and as our two lots of wheat in the Long field and Roberts field would be ripe enough for cutting by Monday or Tuesday, we had to engage the services of neighbours Jack Greene, who also had a reaper-and-binder and the old reliable Paddy Poland, to give us a hand putting up the cap-stooks. Farmers never stooked wheat in the ordinary way like oats and barley, they made cap-stooks instead. These looked like mini stacks with a base of seven or eight sheaves standing as upright as possible against each other. A second row of four or five was then positioned about two feet higher up and capped off with three inverted sheaves. These were tied tightly to each other and the grain heads fanned out to fashion a waterproof cape.

The current "Offaly Independent" for Saturday, the twenty sixth of August advised us the country had been experiencing one of the sunniest spells of the year. We had all our corn crops cut, the oats already stacked, the wheat in cap-stooks and even though it was Sunday and Killeigh hurlers playing Tullamore, we were collared to help stacking our three lots of barley. Out in the field Grandad observed with a fair deal of accuracy,

"We appear to have plenty o' help."

Indeed we had too. Christy, Mick and I were "carryin' in stooks" to Tom Casey and Mother, who made the stacks, while Grandad busied himself with a rake "gatherin' up heads" and pushing them in underneath the band of a sheaf. Needless to say it was beyond the capabilities of any of the young folk to actually carry a full stook but with four of us, continually ferrying two or three sheaves at a time, we had no trouble keeping a constant supply on hand for the two stack makers. Carryin' in stooks was the terminology used to describe this supply line. If performed by young adults or grown-ups they had no great difficulty in grabbing the heads of the four or six sheaves making up the stook and manhandling them, in one lot, over to where the stack was being assembled.

Making the stack properly so as to ensure it didn't slip, let in rainwater or settle skeow-ways, called for special know-how. Unlike the case with cap-stooks, no farmer wanted to see cornfields with stacks on such good terms as to be nodding towards each other. It seemed more or less par for the course for cap-stooks to settle a little skeow-ways and sometimes had to be straightened up if the tilt appeared too extreme. Stacks, on the other hand were made from a solid base, starting off by building round a stook until the outside row of sheaves rested at an acute angle to the ground. Then it progressed upwards, firmly building row upon row until the stack reached about six feet in height. At that point it was headed off with four inverted sheaves tied tightly to each other by their own stalk strands. As with the cap-stooks, the grain heads were then fanned out to act as a shower-proof cape.

We worked until late on Sunday evening and Monday afternoon saw the job finished. All our corn crops were now cut and saved but while thus engaged on Sunday, we missed the second round Junior hurling match in Killeigh between Killeigh and Tullamore. By all accounts an extraordinary game with the Killeigh team made up mostly of two families, the Mahons of Killurin and the Sheerans of Ballinvalley, winning by six goals and one point to no score. Of course we were disgruntled at not being there to witness such a fine win for our parish. However, from an early age we understood only too well, that in harvest time, saving the corn crop came before all else.

These days Grandad and many of our neighbours are talking a lot about Hitler, about Germany and about war. The "Offaly Independent" each week appeals for peace. Young lads, older than us but still just in their late teens or early twenties are joining the L.D.F., the Local Defence Force. Most large meadow or grazing fields in the parish have, by Government Order, been staked with dozens of stout wooden poles driven into the earth at varying distances apart. The reason we are told is to prevent aircraft from landing. Although there is a general air of foreboding, we notice everything still seems to be going ahead in a normal way. Corn is being cut and saved, hay and turf drawn home and farmers in some cases preparing to draw in corn for threshing.

"Sure if there's goin' to be a war, there's goin' to be a war," said Mother, "nobody will be able to stop that ould fella, Hitler."

"An' what's goin' to happen to us, Mammy, if there's a war?" enquired Mick.

"Ah, sure De Valera wont let it come here," answered Grandad, "but we might have to do without tay an' tabackey an' things like that."

"I'd be worried about the tay," quipped Christy, "I wouldn't like to lose that, but I wouldn't be too bothered about the tabackey."

"Go 'long, ye whelp," said Grandad, good humouredly, "what about yer poor ould grandfather?, he wouldn't last long if he hadn't the fillins o' the ould dugeen."

"It's prayin' for peace, ye should be instead of worryin' about tay and tabackey," suggested Mother, "if Hitler comes this way, ye'll have somethin' more to worry about."

13   Drawing in the Sheaves

The good weather lasted almost to the end of the month. There were still many acres of ripe golden corn, to be cut and saved throughout the country.   Just as well all crops don't come to maturity during the same week. If they did there wouldn't be enough reapers-and-binders to handle the situation and quite an amount of grain would be destroyed. The ripening process varied from area to area, even from field to field, depending on the quality of the soil, the quality of the seed, the date of the month on which it was sown and many other factors. And then with barley, as Charlie Kelly often pointed out, "When ye think barley 's ripe, give it another week."

Finches, linnets, sparrows, crows and all seed loving birds are having their own field day garnering the rich harvest of oat and wheat kernels nestling in the stubble of newly cut grain fields. A small lodged area in an uncut wheat crop seems to be the star attraction for a raiding party of woodquests. They home in on the readily accessible grain and then just as quickly, take flight in an explosion of flapping wings when disturbed. The dragonfly or Devil's needle, as we call him, still hovers in the August sun as if monitoring the slow, cumbersome movement of the Autumn-tired wasps, clumsily attempting to feed on over-ripe blackberries. On the bog, this year's brood of young grouse, now grown strong and hardy, show their paces as they sweep low over the contours of brown heather clumps.

We are now into the second week of September and the weather is still holding good. The dog days of burning hot sun are over. The forenoons have that fresh Autumn coolness. The days are calm and warm, ideal harvest conditions and perfect time to gather mushrooms in the early morning dew.

"Pick the mushrooms at the crack o' dawn, whin ye see them," Grandad always said.

"Don't lave the small ones to get bigger, because they won't be there whin ye come back, the fairies 'll have taken them." And sure enough, on the few occasions when we did leave tiny ones to grow bigger, they were not there when we returned later to check.

The warm days still tempt the swallows to fly high but more and more they tend to join their cousins, the house martins, on the telegraph wires, contemplating the long journey back to some African country for warmer winter feeding grounds. There is a good crop of apples on the old arthritic limbed trees in the ould garden and the two damson plum trees beside the mangold pit are bending under the weight of their purple fruit. Horse chestnuts that have broken loose from their green, spiny covers shine like outsize marbles of french polished oak, favourites of all schoolboys in their quest for superiority in the ever-popular conker contests. Bees are still busy rushing home their final collections of honey from the few remaining wild flowers still in bloom.

"We're very lucky with the weather, here," said Grandad, "I was talkin' to a Kilkenny man who wint up to the hurlin' match in Croke Park last Sunday, an' he towld me it was played in a heavy thunderstorm with a lot o' lightnin' ."

"Sure we read all about that on the paper," answered Mother, "an it wasn't last Sunday it was last Sunday week, the third of September, the same day as England declared war on Germany."

"Be the hevers o' war!, I was sure it was last Sunday," added Grandad.

"I must be gettin' ould, the days are goin' by so quick," he continued, "anyway, Kilkenny won, they bate Cork by a point."

Changing the subject, Mother suggested, "We 'll soon have to think about drawin' in the corn, it's stooked and stacked a good while now."

Drawing in the corn and storing it in the haggard in ricks and knee-stacks in preparation for the threshing was a major operation. It was labour intensive and certainly called on a fair amount of muscle. One man and possibly a helper took up position in the field to pitch sheaves, two more with horses and carts, drew in to the haggard and then an experienced rick maker to complete the final act. After much coaxing and cajoling Mother persuaded her brothers, Mike and Tom to start operations on Wednesday. She had already got the nod from Paddy Poland and Tom Clear that they would be available.

On the Monday and Tuesday, Christy, Mick, Tim and I got the job of pulling buachalans in all the grazing fields. For some reason, this year, we were a little apprenhesive about starting the task.   We had heard in school that the buachalan which of course is the common yellow flowered ragworth was very special to the fairies. Anyway we did the job, had good fun and although we considered we didn't believe in fairies still an air of unease persisted. Could our action in some way upset the "good people?."   Could there be any grain of truth in that little poem we learned at school? After all, the following two lines seemed to carry a lot of weight:-

Some call it a weed, and a weed it may be.
But not to the fairies, the buachalan bui.

And then again:-

With bridles and saddles, and stirrups of gold,
They travel through Erin with few to behold,
'Til the first spears of dawning, steal in from the sea,
Then homeward they jog on the buachalan bui.

"For heaven's sake have a titter o' wit," said Mother, "whatever about the fairy tree in the Turn field ye need have no worries about the buachalans, sure haven't we pulled them every year without any problems."

She didn't really convince us but we did carry on and pulled the lot, leaving them in piles along the headland to be burned later when they dried out and died.

Wednesday morning was our big day. Tom and Mike Casey arrived on their bicycles together, followed soon afterwards by Paddy Poland and Tom Clear. Tom Casey, with Christy and Mick as helpers, took the responsibility of one horse and cart. Paddy Poland with me as his side-kick, drove the second. Tom Clear got the job as pitcher in the field and master rick maker of many years, Mike Casey, accepted his favourite role in the haggard.

"Better draw the wheat first, it's the most important crop," said Mike, as he scattered a few forksful of last year's straw over the ground, to serve as a base for the new corn rick.

"Well accordin' to the ould rhyme, the whate is not the most important," said Paddy Poland, jokingly.

"What the hell ould rhyme are ye talkin' about?"

enquired Mike.

"Ye know it as well as I do," answered Paddy, as he slowly recited:-

> The wheat is like a rich man,
> Sleek and well-to-do.
> The oats is like a pack of girls,
> Laughing and dancing too.
> The rye is like a miser,
> Sulky, lean and small,
> But, Oh my boys, the barley
> Is monarch of them all.

"Well, Be the hevers o' war, as "Ould Geg" says, I think I'll have to agree with ye," remarked Mike.

"Of coorse ye will," said Paddy, "sure barley makes the malt, and malt makes the whiskey."

Indeed we all knew wheat had the heaviest sheaves and then maybe it was a good idea as Mike suggested to handle it at the outset, we might have less energy later in the week.

Driving out to the wheat field we hoped some of the knowledge and expertise gained last year concerning load making would have stuck. Nothing caused more annoyance and embarrassment to the seasoned load maker than that his load should slip on the journey back to the haggard. However, we young folk didn't fit into the category of experienced load builders, but somehow, did turn in a clean sheet at this operation last year. To us the most annoying aspect of a slipping load was the delay it might cause while re-loading.

As the two carts arrived in the field at the same time,

Tom Casey left his horse to graze on the headland and decided to assist Tom Clear with the first load. Armed with a two-grained fork he pitched the sheaves up to Paddy and me, who stayed aboard. We filled the centre of the cart with the first lot and then commenced to lay the sheaves in rows, butts outwards, protruding about seven or eight inches over the sideboards, right down along either side. This foundation we carefully squared off by filling the remaining gaps at the front and rear of the cart. Then followed layer upon layer as we built right around the square base, always filling the centre area, to bind the outside sheaves and keep them stable. The secret being we positioned each new tier so as not to protrude just quite so far as the previous one, hence the load very gradually grew slightly narrower as it progressed upwards. When the pitcher considered the cargo to be high enough for safety, we placed a final two single rows from back to front, arranged so as to be underneath the two tieing ropes which were thrown across the top from tailboard to shafts, to anchor down the load.

Paddy and I made ourselves comfortable on our lofty perch and headed out of Roberts field on to the road for the short trip back to the haggard. Driving along high above the hedgerow we waved back to the gang as they proceeded to open up the tie bands of another batch of cap-stooks, in readiness to pitch the second load. Before we left, Grandad had hobbled into the field carrying a long handled wooden rake and as usual busied himself gatherin' up heads. This consisted of raking over the spaces from where the cap-stooks were removed and either making a new sheaf from his rakings or pushing them in underneath the bands of existing sheaves as he gathered them.

During the morning it seemed an easy matter

pitching the wheat down to Mike Casey but by evening time the rick level had grown to be on a par with the top layer of the full load which meant the sheaves at the bottom of the cart had to be thrown up a considerable height to reach the rick maker.

"Just as well those two-grained forks have good long handles," said Paddy, "or I'd never get the shaves up to yer uncle."

It served as a lesson in concentration watching Mike, the craftsman, at work. The rick started out as a stook in the centre of the rectangular straw base and then row after row of sheaves added. The angle of each tier, in relation to the ground, becoming more acute until with the perimeter row almost flat the complete rectangle was covered. Then in a kneeling posture, and handling each sheaf individually he added layer after layer pressing each one neatly and firmly into position with his knee.

By late afternoon the following day all the wheat had been drawn in from both areas, Roberts field and The long field. For the final heading-off of the rick we employed the stratagem of an age old practice, using two loads of sheaves. Tom Casey remained on top of his load while Paddy Poland fed him with sheaves from the other cart then using his lofty vantage point, Tom pitched them on to Mike high up on the rick. With the final sheaf in position Paddy and Tom used an extra tall wooden ladder to ferry up forksful of straw to Mike, to even off the capping. He then threw several weighted twine ropes across the top, to hold the straw secure, in the event of wind.

Mike lingered for a short while on the topmost rungs of the ladder as if just surveying his creation with pride and then delivered two or three well directed flourishes of the two-grained fork, to knock into harmony some protruding wayward strands of the "heading-off" straw. Just as Mike dismounted Fantin Kerwin, another rick maker of some repute, was passing by on his way home from Tullamore. He rambled into the haggard with a friendly,

"God save all here, and God bless the work."

"You too, Fantin avick," answered Tom Casey, "Are ye workin' yer way home from town?"

"Aye, begob, I had to go in to get a few sections for the ould mowin' machine blade."

"What the hell would ye be doin' with mowin' machine blades at this time o' the year?" queried Tom, "Surely ye have all yer hay cut an' drawn in by now."

"Hell to yer sowl, o' coorse I have," answered Fantin, "but I'll have to cut that lock o' barley in the small field at the sheeaun with the mower. I'd never get the reaper-and-binder in there." And then turning to me he continued, "An' I'll want you an' Christy to give me a hand bindin' shaves, Tommy."

"Well, we won't let ye down Mr. Kerwin, just tell us when ye 're ready," I answered.

With that, he took me by the hand, saying in the form of an aside, "I only came in to see yer uncle's rick, an' begob, he made a great job of it. Look at that! See the way he drew it out to a lovely wide showlder, an' then tapered it back all the way to the top. Will you ever be as good as that, Gosson?"

"Ah sure ye could do the same yerself Fantin with yer eyes shut," said Mike, answering for me.

While we prepared to put the spare load of sheaves, which Tom used as a pitching platform, into a stack at the end of the rick, Fantin moved off, reminding Christy and me that he would give us a call in two or three days, when he was ready to mow the barley.   By Saturday evening we had all our corn in the haggard. The ricks and knee-stacks of wheat, barley and oats, positioned in two lines opposite each other, so that the distance apart matched exactly the width of the threshing mill, when driven up between them with it's pitching platforms extended.

At last the scene was set, the harvest saved and our big day, - Thrashin' day - almost at hand. From now on it depended on the availability of Amy Hutchinson's mill and engine.   Amy and his crew were operating in the Gorteen/Killurin area and expected to be back in Ballinvalley within the week. In the meantime, life went on as normal. Many neighbours still busy at various stages of harvest operations, some drawing in corn, others stacking in the fields, with the inevitable few cutting crops that were late in ripening.   Dick Hutchinson invested in a new Fordson tractor from G. N. Walsh in Tullamore for £15O and our teacher, Mrs. Dowling, bought her new Ford eight car from the same source for £165. Paddy Fogarty, one of our school pals told us about what his older brother Francie was going to get for all the packs of small playing cards he had collected. These small cards were available in every packet of Gold Flake cigarettes, one in a packet of ten and two cards in the twenty packet. According to Paddy, his brother could get a lady's or gent's chromium wrist watch for eighteen packs or a bicycle dynamo lighting set for seven. Francie had already collected six packs and was hoping, through the intervention of his brother, that we 'd give him a push because he knew all the Caseys, Mike, Tom and Ned were cigarette smokers.

The war, now almost three weeks on, and the people

of Tullamore are finding it difficult coping with the blackout. The rules are strictly enforced, no street lights, no shop signs after nigthtfall and blinds must be used in all shops and homes in the town to prevent light penetrating to the outside. Rural electrification only came to some surrounding villages in the Autumn of 1938, (last year) and now just twelve months later, it is ironic indeed that all our friends and relations in Tullamore, who for years had enjoyed the great benefits of electric light, are now being asked to cover it up or turn it off.

Yesterday, Sunday the twenty fourth of September, Kerry beat Meath by two points in the All Ireland senior football final and today brought the news that threshings were now in full swing all over the country. Good yields being recorded everywhere with some counties reporting the best return for years. We ourselves had just got the excellent news that Amy Hutchinson and his crew would be coming to thresh early on Saturday, the thirtieth of September. On Tuesday, I accompanied Mother to Tullamore to do some extended shopping in preparation for the big day. Hired sacks for grain had to be collected from D. E. Williams and P. & H. Egan, a quarter barrel of single x porter, two or three shoulders of bacon and many other grocery items from Rhattigans. None of these articles would be paid for until after the threshing. While we were in town, Christy and Mick got word to Mike and Tom Casey, of Amy's intended arrival on Saturday. There never seemed to be any necessity to advise neighbours of the big day. They apparently kept up to date on the grapevine and usually appeared to know exactly where Amy was and where he intended going next.

Thrashin' day, always an awe-inspiring thought for us. The noise, the excitement, the massive red mill, the ponderous chugging engine, the yarns the men told, the food, the eggcupsful of porter and the certain prospect of a new pair of leather boots with studs or clegs and metal heel-tips, when the grain was sold. We looked forward to it so much and now in these last few days leading up to the occasion we almost went off our food and barely slept at night. With a sense of relief Christy and I got word on Thursday morning to report to Fantin Kerwin to bind sheaves. He had eventually arranged to cut this little field of barley beside the sheeaun, with his mowing machine and that at least gave us something to occupy our minds and something definite to do.

We paid good attention to Fantin as we watched him adapt his mowing machine to suit the corn cutting operation. He removed the grassboard from the outside end of the finger-beam and fitted in its place, an item known locally as "the goat." The goat, with it's two extended metal guides which looked like a pair of horns facilitated the separation of the crop proper, from the sward being cut. It also assisted

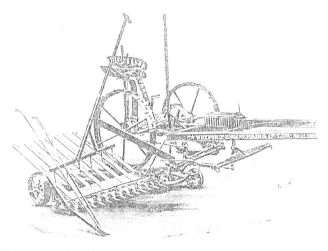

Mowing machine with corn cutting attachment including sheafing-rake. (Courtesy: Wexford County Library)

the barley stalks to fall uniformly on to the lattice table which he hinged to the back edge of the fingerbeam. He then bolted on a second seat, positioned immediately above the ground wheel on the right hand side of the mowing machine. This seat served to accommodate the person in charge of the sheafing rake.

With all systems go, Fantin urged his team into action and set off on the first cut. As the whirring double edged blades sliced into the dry barley stalks they fell in profusion on to the slightly inclined table. Pat Walsh operated the wooden sheafing rake with it's toothed head fitted at an angle of forty five degrees to the handle. When Pat decided he had sufficient corn on the table to make a sheaf he depressed a foot-pedal which flattened the table back against the earth. Simultaneously he exerted pressure with the sheafing rake on the cut stalks. This caused them to slide off the moving table and rest in a neat pile on the stubble ready to be rolled into a sheaf and bound. Fantin drove the machine at a steady pace and this meant Pat

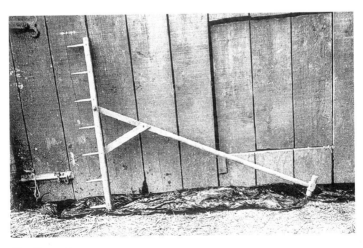

Sheafing rake

213

Walsh's movement of the sheafing rake appeared almost as continuous motion. By the time he pressed one sheaf against the lattice table and let it slide off the next sheaf was ready.

Fantin's daughter Bridgie, joined Christy and me tieing the sheaves. She surveyed our work for a while as we gathered the loose piles in our arms, firmed them up with a dunt of the knee and neatly tied them.

"Begob!" said Bridgie, I must say ye're dab hands at makin' a double band."

"Well why wouldn't we be?", answered Christy, "sure 'twas yer father that first taught us how to do it."

"Aw, well ye couldn't go wrong so," laughed Bridgie, as she tackled the first sheaf herself.

Paddy Walsh came along later to put the sheaves into stooks and by evening time we had the job completed. Fantin had harvested his last remaining field of corn for the year.

With just one day to go, it became more important for us to keep on the move so we busied ourselves all morning, doing and re-doing many of the normal farmyard chores that had either been neglected or partly attended to over recent weeks. Some last minute messages which mother needed were executed without delay. In the afternoon a gang of us including Margaret and Tim, did a circuit of the hazel trees in the first field, the nook and the new garden gathering hazel nuts into jam jars to store away for Halloween. In our enthusiasm it didn't seem to matter that some of the nuts were not quite ripe enough to pull.

After tea, the night wore on tiresomely. We didn't know how to occupy ourselves, it seemed somewhat like waiting for Santa Claus in younger years. Mother and eldest sister Mary were engrossed in the throes of baking bread and generally preparing cutlery and delph for the daunting catering task ahead. There was a continual low-level bickering and teasing going on between the rest of us. Eventually, Mother lost patience and ordered us all to bed. Hard to imagine, but we accepted the order with grace, and in some strange way it acted as a release of tension.

"Ye're goin' to look like right gazebos in the mornin', when I call ye at seven o' clock to open the gap," she said, looking up from the tin basin in which she was mixing a cake and threatening us with a hand covered in dough.

At that moment we knew we'd be better off in bed, we knew we had to get up very early in the morning and above all we knew that, as our mother might say, "tomorrow was the thrashin'."